THE ULTIMATE GUIDE TO

SUCCESSFUL
GUN
TRADING

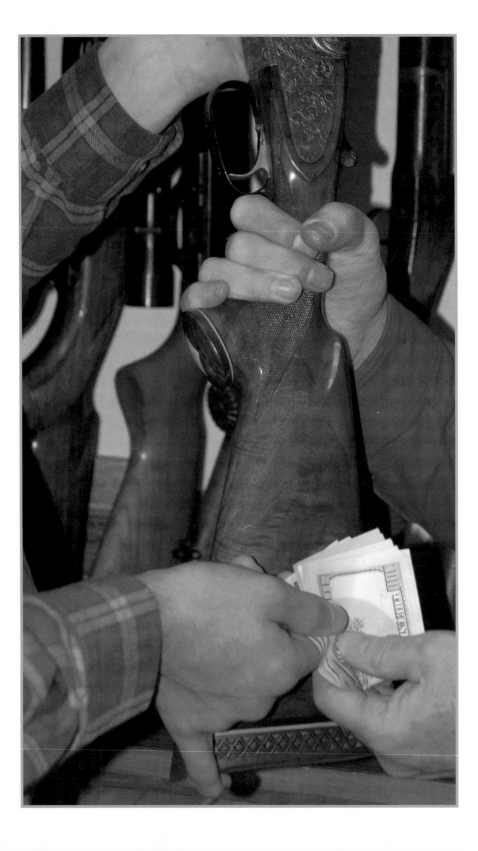

THE ULTIMATE GUIDE TO

SUCCESSFUL
GUN
TRADING

How to Make Money
Buying and Selling Firearms

George Knight

CASTLE BOOKS

DEDICATION

This book draws on experiences, good and bad, accumulated in over half a century of gun tradinging. It is most gratefully dedicated to my wife, Mary Ann, without whose selfless support and relentless encouragement through all of those years it could not have been written, and to Michelle, Suzanne, and Tom, who never objected to Dad's being "out in the shop."

WARNING

The publisher and author advise you to never attempt to disassemble or reassemble a firearm unless you are absolutely certain that it is empty and unloaded. Visually inspect the chamber, the magazine, and firing mechanism to be absolutely certain that no ammunition remains in the firearm. Disassembly and re-assembly should follow the manufacturer's instructions. If such instructions are not immediately available, contact the manufacturer to see if they are available. If they are not available at all, then you should consult other reference sources such as reference books or persons with sufficient knowledge. If such alternative sources are not available and you have a need to disassemble or reassemble the firearm, you should proceed basing your procedures on common sense and experience with similarly constructed firearms.

With regard to the use of these tools, the advice of Brownells, Inc. is generic. For instructions about a specific application, it is best to seek out other sources and not rely solely on the general information and warnings the company provides.

This edition published in 2013 by Castle Books,
A division of BOOK SALES, INC.
276 Fifth Avenue Suite 206
New York, New York 10001
USA

This edition published by arrangement with Skyhorse Publishing, Inc.

10 9 8 7 6 5 4 3 2 1

Library of Congress Cataloging-in-Publication Data is available on file.
ISBN: 978-0-7858-3039-9

Printed in China

TABLE OF CONTENTS

TABLE OF CONTENTS

FOREWORD

What is it that draws people to trading, swapping, bartering and exchanging? There may be a variety of lesser reasons, but I believe that mostly it has to do with "getting the better end of the deal." Regardless of what's being traded, the idea that seems to be the common denominator is one of "coming out ahead."

The goal of this handbook is to put professional guidelines for all aspects of profitably trading firearms together in one place. It explains the basic economics of gun trading and shows you how to set you own objectives, then gives you a complete course in evaluating potential purchases, buying the right way, and selling for maximum return.

This handbook focuses solely on making a profit. Interest in the artistry of the gun, in the history of weaponry and in the mechanics of firearms are all secondary to the gun trader's goal: coming out ahead.

Today's successful gun trader will probably find that he or she is already following the principles outlined in this book. The novice will find it to be a comforting reference that can help keep him "in the black" while he gains the experience necessary to be considered a seasoned gun trader.

With *The Ultimate Guide to Successful Gun Trading*, I offer no "magic." As you read it, you'll see that it is all based on some simple yet powerful ideas, few of them new, but many of them not previously put into print. I make no promises but one: If you will use the TEK evaluation system and consistently apply the ideas and approaches outlined in this book, you will "come out ahead" every time. Trade by trade, deal by deal, you will see your stake grow and grow . . . as large as you are willing to make it.

Welcome to the exciting world of gun trading.

ACKNOWLEDGEMENTS

The author gratefully acknowledges the following, among many others, for their assistance in producing this book:

Peter and Kate Fiduccia, for having the willingness to take a chance on a rookie author; Larry Weeks of Brownells, for his extensive assistance with technical information and product photos; Doug Turnbull of Turnbull Restorations, for his help with beautiful photo examples of the restorer's art; Tim Marchok, for his assistance in getting the "conditions" photos just right; Rick Punderson and Mike Methe, from whom I have learned so much just by watching and listening; Tom Knight, for his continuing thoughts and reviews as this book evolved; and finally, Johnny Sihack, the other half of my very first gun trade in 1951 . . . wherever you may be.

GETTING STARTED...

INTRODUCTION TO GUN TRADING

1. WHAT IS GUN TRADING?

"Gun collecting," "investing in guns," "gun retailing (wholesaling)" and "gun trading" are all activities that involve the acquisition and disposition of firearms, but each has its own set of objectives.

Take "gun collecting" for example; as with any type of collecting, from stamps to butterflies to baseball cards, the idea is to gather into one location a group of guns that are directly related. The collection might focus on a period in history, such as the Revolutionary War, or it could be dedicated to a particular activity, as with military weaponry. The collector might specialize in a style of firearm, for instance double-barreled shotguns, or he might concentrate on a single manufacturer, such as Colt. Whatever the area of interest, the objective is to assemble a group of arms containing at least one of each applicable specimen, and then to upgrade the condition of the individual pieces to the best available. But no matter how large the collection, or how frequent the upgrades, gun collecting is not gun trading.

Gun retailing or wholesaling is plain old retailing focused on a single product, either by itself or as part of a larger grouping, as in a sporting-goods operation. But no matter the volume, gun retailing/wholesaling is not gun trading.

Lastly, let's look at "investing in guns." The typical investor often operates like the collector, gathering a specialized group of guns together. His selection of an area of concentration, however, will usually be dictated by the potential for growth in the value of the collection. This usually leads to a focus on areas like Colts, Winchesters, pre-war American doubles, British/European high-grade doubles, or the rare specialties, like Confederate weapons. The presumption of the investor is that the value of the collection will outpace inflation and will outperform, over time, alternative investments such as stocks, bonds and real estate. Gun investors also often talk about the "psychic income" associated with owning these valuable guns and seeing the collection grow. But even "investing in guns" isn't the same as gun trading.

So if gun trading isn't any of these things, what is it? For the rest of this handbook, we're going to use the following definition: Gun trading is the buying

1

and selling of firearms for the specific purpose of making a targeted profit over the short term.

A gun trader is not a collector, retailer or investor. He will buy any affordable firearm within his area of expertise so long as it meets his criteria for potential short-term profit. He will sell every firearm as soon as his profit objective can be reached, or as soon as it becomes apparent that his objective will not be reached. The gun trader lives for "the action": finding the guns, buying them right, selling them right, and watching the bank account grow. The gun trader treats the gun as a marketable commodity . . . a marvelously interesting, beautiful and enjoyable commodity, but a commodity nonetheless.

The purpose of this handbook is to help you, the gun trader, build your own definitions of "buying right" and "selling right," and to show you how to use those definitions in a disciplined way to maximize your financial returns. Incidentally, gun trading is not synonymous with gun swapping (literally gun trading). While the gun trader may occasionally engage in a swap, it is only a momentary means to an end. We'll talk more about handling a trade situation in a later section, but for now, the only thing we want to trade a gun for is money.

Can you be a gun trader and also be a collector or investor? Well, let's put it this way . . . you can split your time up doing any or all of these things, but there is a danger that your focus will stray from gun trading. If you do decide to be your own best customer, separate your activities and your funds, and treat yourself as you would any other customer.

Of course, gun trading isn't all numbers on a spreadsheet. One very exciting aspect is "the hunt" . . . searching out guns for purchase. Take for example the call I received one Sunday evening. I'd placed a small ad in the local classifieds for "Antique and Modern Arms Bought, Sold and Traded". At about 8 p.m., a lady's thin, but clear, voice said she had seen the ad and had a Colt pistol for sale. She stated that it was in the original box, was marked Colt, and had the number 31 on it.

"What does it say on the end of the box?"

"Nothing. The box isn't marked at all."

"Why do you think that it's the original box?"

"Because the gun fits right into a space and it has other spaces for the tools."

"Would this box be made of cardboard or wood?"

"It's made of wood on the outside and has velvet on the inside."

"Is it too late to come and see you right now?"

My caller agreed to meet with me in about an hour. Since she lived about 30 minutes away, which gave me half an hour to figure out what she had, and decide how much to offer.

I was quite sure that I would be seeing a cased Colt revolver, and guessed that the 31 on the frame was more likely to be the caliber than the serial number. Just a hunch. I quickly ran through my Colt reference, looking for 31 caliber revolvers.

When I rolled down the driveway, I had concluded that the gun in the wooden box might well be a Colt-Root revolver, and I had checked asking prices for that item in a couple of periodicals (this was in the pre-Internet days).

When I arrived, the lady brought out a small wooden case, one edge of which had been repaired. I recall savoring the moment briefly before I opened the box, but when the lid went up, there indeed was a very nice Root revolver with a bullet mold, screwdriver, several lead balls and a partial box of caps. I looked the gun over carefully, then had a decision to make. So far, the lady hadn't mentioned a price. Sensing, again just on a hunch, that I was going to get only one shot at the purchase, I made my maximum offer right up front. She turned to her mother, whose age I guessed at about 60 (I later learned she was 91!) and said, "Well, that's $75 more than the other two men offered, so I believe we should sell it to Mr. Knight." After the transaction had been completed, the mother told me that the gun had been her father's. He had lived in the area all his life and had purchased this Colt when she was a small child.

When I got home, I looked the case and contents over more carefully and realized that the cover of the box of caps was missing, and had been replaced by a wad of crumpled paper. I removed that box of caps, replaced it with another I had on hand, and sold the gun shortly thereafter for just over the anticipated price. I moved the original box of caps around on the bench for several months, until finally, it wound up on the floor. The wad of paper fell out of the box and the caps scattered. While gathering them up, I noticed a printed letter on the paper. When I opened it up, I found it was a receipt, not for the gun, but from a local feed store. It was dated 1891 and made out to the seller's grandfather. This receipt would have added no value to the package, even had I still owned the gun, but it is an example of some of the "added interest" things that can pop up while you are gun-hunting.

2. THE ECONOMICS OF GUN TRADING

The key to successful gun trading is not in the selling, it is in the buying. Buy using the TEK system and the selling will take care of itself.

Think back to our definition of gun trading and you'll remember that it calls for us to "make a targeted profit over the short term." In other words, we want to make a planned amount of money quickly. We'll start off with a known amount in our pocket. When we buy a gun, we'll take money out of the pocket, and when we sell a gun, we'll put the money (all of it!) into the pocket. We'll also have to take some out whenever we spend money in support of buying or selling. The idea is that when we finally turn that pocket inside-out at the end of the week and count the money, we want to have a significantly larger bankroll than when we started.

A COUPLE OF REMINDERS

First, risk and reward are directly opposed to one another. You will never really get "something for nothing." Safe investments are fine, but they "pay low," just like at the casino. A risky investment, that is, one with no guarantee, is viable only when it promises a major return. There is always something that can go wrong with a high-return investment. Otherwise it would not have a high return! Regardless of what anyone may promise, this maxim simply never changes.

Second, about potential returns and cash-in-hand . . . they are not necessarily the same thing. Regardless of how great things look on paper, or in the gun rack, you have not realized the return until the gun has been sold and the funds received. Acquiring the gun is only the first part of the job. The second part is exchanging the gun for the largest number of dollars as quickly as possible. Until the second part is completed, you have only potential return.

So how do we begin? Just as you would begin a vacation trip or a hike, we need to know where we want to wind up before deciding in what direction to start off. For example, if you begin with $100 in your pocket, you might decide that at the end of the day you want to have $150 in your pocket after everything is sold and the bills are paid. Also, you decide that you need to do all this in one month. In financial terms, you want your principal ($100) to grow by $50 (50 percent markup) in one month. This equates to an annualized return to you of 600 percent . . . quite a bit better than the savings rate at your local bank.

Before going further, let's define a couple of terms, because they'll be used again and again in this chapter and they're important to the gun trading concept.

Opportunity cost: Think of this as the return you didn't make because you didn't put your money to work.

Revenue: The total amount of money we received for what we sold. Revenue includes all the money coming in, even if we have to pass some of it along, as with sales taxes.

MARGIN AND MARKUP				
Buy				
$100.00		Margin %	=	Markup %
Sell	Profit			
111.00	11.00	10%		11%
117.65	17.65	15%		18%
125.00	25.00	20%		25%
133.33	33.33	25%		33%
142.86	42.86	30%		43%
153.85	53.85	35%		54%
166.67	66.67	40%		67%
181.82	81.82	45%		82%
200.00	100.00	50%		100%

Margin: The percentage of the selling price that is profit. (Profit as a % of selling price)

Markup: The percentage by which the cost is increased to reach a selling price. (Profit as a % of cost)

Margin: Profit divided by selling price; expressed as a percentage. (See Margin and Markup Table.)

Markup: Profit divided by cost; expressed as a percentage. (See Margin and Markup Table.)

Principal: The amount of money with which we begin. We will also refer to this as our "stake." The idea is to use the principal over and over again to earn a net profit. When we make a profit, we have the option of adding it to the existing stake, keeping it, or doing a little of both. This is also known as re-investing or "plowing back the profits." The larger our stake, the more money we can make.

Gross Profit: This is the difference between the cost of the gun itself and the price for which we sell it. We have to make a gross profit, but by itself, gross profit is not enough. The only thing that matters to us, as gun traders, is "net profit."

Net Profit: From the gross profit, subtract the total of any other money spent, beyond the cost of the gun itself. This is the net profit . . . which goes into our pocket or is added to the stake.

Inflation/Deflation: Quite simply, inflation means that prices in general are going up, while deflation means just the opposite. Inflation, at relatively low levels, is the gun trader's friend. Rampant inflation, such as we saw in the 1978-81 period, can be a problem to the gun trader who doesn't anticipate its ending.

Alternative Uses: Whenever we choose to do one thing with our money, it means not doing other things with that same money. In order to evaluate the wisdom of our choice, we need to understand what else we might have done . . . what alternatives we had:

Do nothing beyond putting the money in a safe or under the mattress. In times of inflation, this approach eliminates any opportunity for the money in hand to grow. Assuming that the money does not burn up or get stolen, you never lose dollars, but you do lose buying power. With that $50, today you can buy 25 gallons of gas. But if gas prices go up tomorrow, while you still have the same $50, it will buy fewer gallons. Of course if prices go down (deflation), the reverse is true . . . the $50 has more buying power. Our objective is to cause the $50 to increase at a rate substantially faster than prices are increasing in general.

Put the funds in a savings account (or equivalent). This is a very safe alternative, often insured by the government, and your rate of return is usually guaranteed. The down side, of course, is that the return is always very low because the risk of loss is very low.

Invest in established markets, such as stocks and bonds, which offer a higher return because of the higher risk of loss. In these markets, the folks who know the most make the most. Often these are the market specialists, the portfolio managers and the brokers. Those of us who go to them for advice or investment services get a significantly lower return.

Real estate is one of the best-known "non-financial" alternative ways to invest your money. Stories abound in which a piece of ground was purchased for a song and sold almost immediately to the railroad, to an oil developer, to Mega-Mart, etc.

Most deals are much less lucrative, and some are downright losers. The upside: There's no more land being made, and everybody wants some. The downside: Much of it is where no one really wants it, usually involves a good chunk of cash, generally requires a long time to find out whether you guessed right or not, and consequently, is subject to an awful lot of things that can go wrong.

Finally, we come to the "individual expertise transaction," and this is what gun trading is all about. You bet your money that you know more about the gun and the market than the next guy does. These would generally be classified as high-risk transactions because there are absolutely no guarantees involved. Get it right and you're a hero, but get it wrong and you're a bum. So here's where to pay attention! You are going to dramatically reduce that risk by being knowledgeable about the subject matter, and further reduce it by employing the two-level TEK selection system. In this way, you bring the risk down to a level where it is far outweighed by the return, and good gun traders are doing just that every day.

Why does knowledge reduce the risk? Risk is basically the chance of something going wrong, and knowledge eliminates many of the things that might go wrong.

For example . . . you are considering buying a shotgun: Some of the risks would be along the lines of damage, incorrect parts, poor condition or an illegal configuration. Other risks might involve your assessment of the demand for the gun. The final risks would be physical: rust, handling damage, theft. You are going to become an expert, and in every instance, your expertise – what constitutes a correct part or condition . . . a legal configuration (barrel at least 18″, etc.) . . . proper storage and handling . . . the current market for this particular gun – will eliminate most of the potential buying and selling errors.

Turnover: Turnover is to a gun trader what speed is to a hockey forward, or a good arm is to a pitcher or a quarterback. You can play the game without it, but you'll work harder and win less often. Let me show you why.

Example 1: I take $1,200 from my savings account and buy 12 rifles, selling them at the end of a year for $150 each. I have my $1,200 back, total sales of $1,800 and I've made a profit of $600. Seems like a pretty good deal. I made $600 on an investment of $1,200 in one year.

Example 2: Let's say that I take only $100 out of my savings account and buy only one .22 rifle. In four weeks, I sell the gun for $150, giving back to me the original $100, plus another $50 in profit. I put the $50 in my back pocket. I then take the remaining $100 and go out and buy another .22 rifle, sell it in four weeks for $150, and keep repeating this cycle for a year. After that 12th transaction, my totals for the year would be sales of $1,800 (12 x $150), cost of guns sold = $1,200 (12 x $100), and a gross profit of $600 (12 x $50).

At least on the surface, this appears to be the same result as in the first scenario, except that I had to do more work. So how could this be a better outcome than Example 1?

Example 3: I do the same thing as in Example 1, except that I sell each gun in two weeks instead of four. After the 12th cycle, I have the original stake back, the

Three Examples of the Power of Turns

	Example 1	Example 2	Example 3
Cost per Gun	100	100	100
Sale price per gun	150	150	150
Profit per gun	50	50	50
Total sales	1800	1800	1800
Total profit	600	600	600
No. of transactions	1	12	12
Elapsed time	12 months	12 months	6 months
Average investment	1200	100	100
Annual turns	1	12	24
Margin per transaction	33.3%	33.3%	33.3%
Annualized Margin	33.3%	400.0%	800.0%

Here is a comparison of the three examples given in the text. Although the first four lines of each example are the same, notice what happens to the other lines as you increase the turn rate.

same volume of sales and the same profit, just like the first two examples. Looks like I had to do the same work as in Example 2, but even faster. I did it all in only 6 months . . . yet I still only had $600 to show for it. This could be a better way to go?

The table above summarizes the details of each example for comparison. Notice that the first five lines are the same for all three examples. The differences in the outcomes become apparent as you scan the bottom half of the chart.

If you've already figured out that the most favorable outcome is Example 3, you're well on your way to understanding the power of turnover. Example 3 is the best because you have your $600 profit in only six months instead of a year. This is important because now you can go out and do the same thing for another six months and finish the year with a $1,200 profit on your original $100 investment. You would be "turning over" your original stake ($100) 24 times, or to put it another way, you would have a "turn rate" of 24. Sure, you worked harder, but that is one of the underlying themes of this book. You work hard, but you get paid according to how hard you work. If you believe that you should get a high return without putting out the effort, you'll need to change that approach if this line of endeavor is going to work for you. The returns from gun trading can be handsome, but you will earn them.

What can we say about the first two examples? In Example 1, the turn rate is one because you turned your original $1,200 stake over only one time during the

Stake $100

THE MAGIC OF TURNS

NUMBER OF TURNS PER YEAR											
1	2	3	4	5	6	7	8	9	10	11	12

MARGIN	YOUR PROFIT WOULD BE											
10%	11	22	33	44	56	67	78	89	100	111	122	133
15%	18	35	53	71	88	106	124	141	159	176	194	212
20%	25	50	75	100	125	150	175	200	225	250	275	300
25%	33	67	100	133	167	200	233	267	300	333	367	400
30%	43	86	129	171	214	257	300	343	386	429	471	514
35%	54	108	162	215	269	323	377	431	485	538	592	646
40%	67	133	200	267	333	400	467	533	600	667	733	800
45%	82	164	245	327	409	491	573	655	736	818	900	982
50%	100	200	300	400	500	600	700	800	900	1000	1100	1200

	13	14	15	16	17	18	19	20	21	22	23	24
10%	144	156	167	178	189	200	211	222	233	244	256	267
15%	229	247	265	282	300	318	335	353	371	388	406	424
20%	325	350	375	400	425	450	475	500	525	550	575	600
25%	433	467	500	533	567	600	633	667	700	733	767	800
30%	557	600	643	686	729	771	814	857	900	943	986	1029
35%	700	754	808	862	915	969	1023	1077	1131	1185	1238	1292
40%	867	933	1000	1067	1133	1200	1267	1333	1400	1467	1533	1600
45%	1064	1145	1227	1309	1391	1473	1555	1636	1718	1800	1882	1964
50%	1300	1400	1500	1600	1700	1800	1900	2000	2100	2200	2300	2400

Here is another example of how turns will make your money grow, even if you don't plow the profits back into the business. For an opening stake of $100, each column shows the profit earned at a given margin and a given turn rate. Notice the number of different ways in which a given profit, say $200, can be achieved.

year. In Example 2, the turn rate is 12, because you reused that $100 over again each month. Since the sales and the profits are the same in both cases, the only difference is the turn rate. What difference does the turn rate make? Just this: In Example 2, you only needed a $100 stake to get going, whereas in Example 1, you needed $1,200. So if you had only $100, and were planning to follow the second example, you wouldn't even have been able to get started.

But if you did have the $1,200, and you followed Example 2, you would have purchased 12 guns at the beginning, sold them all four weeks later for $150 each, bought 12 more, sold them in a month, etc. At the end of the year with this turn rate of 12, your sales would be $21,600 and your profit would be $7,200 . . . all from that $1,200 stake. Same turn rate as Example 2 and same profit margin, just 12 times more money . . . because you started with a stake that was 12 times larger.

To see even more clearly how the power of turns can make your money grow, look at the "Magic of Turnover" (See The Magic of Turns Table above). It demonstrates what happens to a stake of $100 turned over from one to 24 times in a year on sales yielding margins of 10 percent-50 percent.

Turnover is an idea that we can use to make a good thing better, but sometimes we need to focus on turns to make something work at all. Consider the following:

1. The smaller our stake, the more we need high turnover to make a sizeable profit in a given period. Higher turns generate profit over a shorter period of time, allowing us to plow that profit back into our stake, creating more profit, etc.

2. The larger our stake, the more we need high turnover to cover the "opportunity cost" of the stake. Remember the example where we had $1,200 available to buy that group of .22 rifles? There were probably some other opportunities available for us to invest that same $1,200, most or all of which weren't open to us when we had only $100. The larger our stake, the more we can do with it, so higher turn rates can allow gun trading to show better overall returns than those alternatives.

3. A higher turn rate is an effective way to compensate for a lower profit margin. Making $50 of profit in one week is the same as making $200 of profit in a month provided that we keep the $50 working. $50 is not equal to $200, but $50 made four times in a month is the same as $200 made once a month. And if it takes even one day longer than a month to make that $200, making $50 for each of four weeks is more profitable.

4. Rapid turnover preserves our options for more buying and protects against inventory damage or loss. Let's say you put most of your stake into a group of guns that will give you your target margin, but will take a while to sell. Granted, you took that longer sell time into account when making your offer, but time is still time. Halfway through your planned sell time, along comes another group of guns for sale. Compared with what you purchased, these have a higher level of demand, a more rapid turn potential, and promise a better profit margin . . . but your stake is all tied up. Had you been able to achieve a higher turn rate, you would be in a position to at least make an offer on this more attractive group. The message here is that just because you bought the guns at a price that anticipated a longer sale time, there is no reason not to do everything you can to beat that deadline. Don't ever let up on efforts for making the sale happen just because your "window for sale" still has plenty of time left. Remember Murphy's Law. The more rapidly you turn over your stock, the less likely it is to be damaged or "lost," because for any given stake level, your average in-stock position will always decline as your turn rate grows. Get it in and move it out.

5. Rapid turnover can actually help create the next "buying opportunity" because it forces you to be "out there" looking for one. By being "out there," you are more likely to be in the right place at the right time. (Remember, the secret is not just in turning the money over, it's in turning it over repeatedly.) This is an important difference between a true gun trader and someone who just buys a used gun every so often.

3. THE TEK SYSTEM

The TEK purchase-evaluation system is a technique for quickly and unemotionally reviewing a potential gun trading purchase. TEK stands for Turns, Effort and Knowledge, the three major components of the system, and it uses a profile that you set up to reflect your own desires for price range, turnover rate, and profit level and risk. You can change your profile as quickly as you can change your mind. Once your profile is set up, you'll be equipped with three things (along with your "funds") that will go with you as you search for purchase opportunities.

NICHE KNOWLEDGE

First of all, you'll carry your "niche knowledge" with you. Everywhere we look today, we see businesses, from major corporations to individual proprietors, finding their specific area of business interest, or niche. You rarely find a General Store today, one selling everything from cornmeal to underwear to shovels. Retailers are specialists, such as health-food stores for special cornmeal, lingerie and men's shops for underwear, and specialty catalogs for special shovels with ergonomic handles, etc. Even that great General Store called Wal-Mart is a niche seller. Their niche is the low-price, high-volume business. If is doesn't fit that description, they don't handle it.

So, too, with you as a gun trader and this cannot be over-emphasized. You will trade only within your area of expertise . . . your "knowledge niche." You will be completely familiar with the market price, demand level and the scarcity factor for your specialties, and you'll know how to recognize proper markings, features and conditions. Of course, this doesn't all have to be committed to memory. You will have an extensive set of reference materials to use, and you'll probably put together a series of quick-check notes in a small carrying format. If you are a quick study, you will be able to absorb the available material on a particular model quite quickly. This is the beauty of a good reference library.

For example, I recently had a Springfield 1903 rifle offered to me for purchase. My first reaction when it came out of the case was that it was a well-done home-sporterized version of the military model, even though it was rather plain and somewhat heavy. But because it was in very nice condition, I did some homework on it before making the offer. It turned out to be a Springfield Sporter, an arm I had read about but hadn't previously encountered. Fortunately, I have an excellent Springfield reference on the shelf, and in a few minutes found the information I needed to properly evaluate the gun. If I find myself considering another Sporter, I won't feel like an expert, but I'll know what to look for without going back to the books. As you gain experience, you will increase your niche knowledge, and in fairly short order, you will find yourself able to evaluate almost everything that comes your way.

Don't let this idea of becoming an expert in your niche area scare you. You don't need to know everything about every firearm ever made. You only need to be familiar with the facts that influence the price you will pay for the gun. If you want to deal in Winchester 94's, you need to understand features and dates of manufacture. If you are considering Colt revolvers, you'll want to be aware of generations, finishes and options. On the other hand, for many guns, there really isn't a lot to learn beyond the basics. It will be easy to learn and remember the details of the guns you like, but stretch yourself beyond "likes" to get into the pieces that don't particularly appeal to you. I urge you to push yourself this way so that you don't arbitrarily give up the profit opportunities associated with a wider knowledge niche.

CSD RATING

Secondly, you will be armed with a "CSD rating" (Condition, Scarcity, and Demand) rating that will reflect the minimum levels of these factors acceptable to you. Anything not making your profile's minimum grade will be dropped from consideration, unless it is ridiculously under-priced (remembering at the same time that deals that seem too good to be true usually are). If a potential purchase does make your clip level, the CSD number is used to determine the price you will offer for the gun, as we will demonstrate later.

DISCOUNT PERCENTAGE

Finally, you'll have a "discount percentage," representing the reduction from full retail value that will determine your maximum offering price. This percentage will be determined by your profile and by the CSD rating of the gun. It's like mentally drawing a line in the sand. You adopt a disciplined approach that says you simply won't go beyond thus and such a price. This will keep you from getting "caught up" in the deal-making process . . . and you won't be upset with the seller if he or she doesn't go along.

Notice that we have not talked about an actual buying price yet. That's because even if your profile doesn't change, the size of the stake you have available at any one point in time may go up or down. We simply apply the TEK approach to any potential purchases within the range of our stake. Obviously you won't waste time on developing an opportunity which, even if you buy it at the TEK-suggested price, would cost more than your available stake.

Now you might ask, "Why not at least take a shot at buying it on the cheap?" There are two reasons for not doing so. The first simply is that the odds are against your being successful, and we have much better places to spend the time. Remember that gun trading is as much about time as it is about money. The second reason is that "low-balling" is the mark of an amateur. It is a tactic which may work from time to time, particularly on the unknowing, but it doesn't take long for a reputation to get started, and that can hurt you big-time with other potential sellers who do understand the business.

Now let's look at these three things in more detail and start developing your profile.

4. ESTABLISHING YOUR PROFILE

There is no such thing as a "correct" TEK profile. We aren't trying to tag you with a number. In building your TEK profile, we are going to try to decide how much time you want to spend on gun trading and how much risk you feel comfortable with. We'll also look at the demands you want to place on your money, recognizing that the harder it works, the more that will be required in terms of effort and risk acceptance on your part (recall what we said earlier about reducing that risk through knowledge).

The key question to be asked in forming your profile is, "How hard am I willing to work?" Will gun trading provide the major portion of your income, or will it still be a "second job." This is important because you'll find there are many people chasing the guns coming onto the market. You'll be reviewing and discarding many purchase opportunities for each one you accept. Since the bulk of the accepted chances will probably not be found at organized events like gun shows, you'll have to work hard to keep the next buys in the pipeline coming. Like a good chess player, you'll always be looking several moves ahead. That takes time, energy and creativity on your part, but the harder you work your money and yourself, the more money you will have to work with.

Your profile can and will change over time, depending on where you want to push it. Once you understand how the various TEK Grid elements work with one another, you'll position yourself at the "minimum-risk" end, or at the "maximum-gain" end, or, like most of us, at a point in between.

5. THE TEK GRID

Completely understand this grid and you will understand why TEK works.

CSD Sieve Size:

This is the starting point for the grid. The sieve "size" is the minimum number of total CSD points you will require for accepting a transaction. Just as with a real sieve or screen, the smaller (tighter) the holes, the fewer the items that will pass through for your use. If you choose to be a "high grader," that is, you want only scarce material in fine condition and in high demand, you will obviously have to look harder and longer to find it, and each piece may be expensive.

At the other end of the stick, if you decide to consider anything above a very low CSD total, you should have no trouble putting stock on your sales rack. However, you'll find you have to work much harder to find buyers for the poorer-conditioned material. Some or most of your stake will be tied up in low-demand items, and you may also have to work on lower margins, which means pushing extra hard to hit your turn target. At certain times and in certain areas, you'll simply have to work with what is available, but always try to work as far up the CSD scale as you can, even though that will mean buying fewer pieces for any given stake size.

"Readily Available Buys" refers to the number of guns you look at, not the price of those guns. The volume of buy opportunities is directly proportional to effort and creativity on your part. The harder you work, and the more ideas you come up with for sources, the more guns you will come across and the more opportunities you will have to keep your pipeline full. Having enough material to work with is a fundamental requirement for your success with the TEK system.

Keeping the Stake Working:

The more acceptable opportunities you encounter, the more likely you are to keep your stake fully invested. If your stake isn't invested, it cannot make money for you.

Stake Impact:

The farther up on the CSD scale you work, the more impact each buy will have on your stake because individual purchases will generally be more expensive. TEK works the same no matter how much or how little money you have to begin with (your stake). It is true that the smaller your stake, the more potential buys you'll have to pass up, but you will still be making money at the same rate as you would be with a larger stake. And if you elect to plow most or all of your profits back into the stake, you'll move up quickly.

Stake Impact is also included in the grid because we want to recognize that a small stake may initially prevent us from playing exclusively in the high-end CSD bracket. Again, though, work as high on the CSD scale as you can.

Readily Available Sales:

High CSD point guns sell more easily than low-point guns. You may have to look harder for your buyer, but there will be less sales resistance when you find him. The deciding factor is whether he can afford the gun, not whether or not it is worth the money.

Discount from Retail:

Discount is important at all CSD levels, but especially if you elect to operate in the low CSD rating areas. This is because purchases at this level will undoubtedly include guns with low demand numbers and/or low condition numbers. (Selectively rejecting low-demand and/or low-condition guns is equivalent to raising your CSD rating.)

If you are working the low end of CSD, you must use a high discount rate to protect your turns target. Note what we just said: The high discount rate is needed to protect your turns target, not to provide you with more profit. That is, in order to turn the low CSD guns promptly, you must hold the selling price down to offset low demand, and/or as compensation for poorer condition. Once again, the higher discount rate is not intended to provide more profit, but to allow you to sell far enough below retail to make your planned profit within your planned turn timeframe.

Hitting Your Turns Target:

Turns are the magic ingredient of the TEK system. Whether you plan to make a lot every so often, or make less but do it more frequently, hitting your turns target is the primary objective. As noted above, guns from the higher levels of the CSD point scale are "easier" to turn because you will meet less sales resistance. Your audience

TEK SYSTEM GRID FACTORS

Col 1 CSD SIEVE SIZE	Col 2 READILY AVAILABLE BUYS	Col 3 KEEPING STAKE WORKING	Col 4 STAKE IMPACT	Col 5 READILY AVAILABLE SALES	Col 6 DISCOUNT FROM RETAIL	Col 7 HITTING TURNS TARGET
TIGHT 12 POINTS	FEWER	HARDER	HIGH	MANY	LOW	EASIER
9 POINTS						
6 POINTS						
OPEN 3 POINTS	MANY	EASIER	LOW	FEWER	HIGH	HARDER

As the sieve size in Col 1 tightens, there are corresponding changes that occur in Cols 2-7. Notice the inverse relationships between Columns 2 and 5, between Columns 3 and 7, and between Columns 4 and 6. Be sure to understand why these relationships are true, because they clearly demonstrate that the harder you work, the more money you will be able to make.

of prospective buyers will change significantly as you move up the CSD scale.

There are two TEK discount tables. They are the same in format, but they assume different levels of expertise on the part of the user. TEK-1 has built-in insurance against making a poor evaluation of the condition and/or market value of a gun. Using TEK-1, you may make a smaller percentage of the potential buys you attempt, but those are quite likely to turn out well. I strongly recommend that you use TEK-1 until you are thoroughly familiar with the ins and outs of gun trading.

The TEK-2 assumes that you have very accurately pegged the gun in terms of condition, scarcity, and demand, and that you are facing significant competition in your area from other experienced gun traders. It reflects the idea that you are able, and required, to accept a higher level of risk to reach your trading objectives. ∎

THE TEK-I TABLE

1. Your total CSD Pts	2. So Plan to sell at (% of Retail)	3. If Your Desired Margin Is								
		10%	15%	20%	25%	30%	35%	40%	45%	50%
		4. Your Maximum Offer Should Be This Percentage of Market								
13-15	95%	86%	81%	76%	71%	67%	62%	57%	52%	48%
10-12	85%	77%	72%	68%	64%	60%	55%	51%	47%	43%
7-9	75%	68%	64%	60%	56%	53%	49%	45%	41%	38%
4-6	55%	50%	47%	44%	41%	39%	36%	33%	30%	28%
0-3	40%	36%	34%	32%	30%	28%	26%	24%	22%	20%

To use this table to determine your offering price, do the following: In section 1, locate the line that reflects the total CSD points you have assigned the gun. The corresponding line in section 2 shows the discount from market at which you will plan to sell the gun. Move across to section 4, on the same line, until you intersect the column of section 3 that reflects the margin you want to make on the sale. (This is the margin number developed in your profile.) The number at the intersection of these two lines is the maximum percentage of market that you should offer for the gun.

THE TEK-II TABLE

1. Your total CSD Pts	2. So Plan to sell at (% of Retail)	3. If Your Desired Transaction Margin Is								
		2%	3%	4%	5%	6%	7%	8%	9%	10%
		4. Your Maximum Offer Should Be This Percentage of Retail								
13-15	95%	93%	92%	91%	90%	89%	88%	87%	86%	86%
10-12	90%	88%	87%	86%	86%	85%	84%	83%	82%	81%
7-9	85%	83%	82%	82%	81%	80%	79%	78%	77%	77%
4-6	70%	69%	68%	67%	67%	66%	65%	64%	64%	63%
0-3	50%	49%	49%	48%	48%	47%	47%	46%	46%	45%

TURNS PER YEAR	ANNUALIZED MARGIN								
6	12%	18%	24%	30%	36%	42%	48%	54%	60%
7	14%	21%	28%	35%	42%	49%	56%	63%	70%
8	16%	24%	32%	40%	48%	56%	64%	72%	80%
9	18%	27%	36%	45%	54%	63%	72%	81%	90%
10	20%	30%	40%	50%	60%	70%	80%	90%	100%
11	22%	33%	44%	55%	66%	77%	88%	99%	110%
12	24%	36%	48%	60%	72%	84%	96%	108%	120%

The TEK-II table is used in the same manner as the TEK-I table. The margins are designed to achieve an acceptable annualized total, rather than focusing on the individual transaction. The corresponding annualized margin value is shown at the bottom of the TEK-II columns. As noted in the text, use the TEK-I table for your work unless competition for purchases forces you to the riskier TEK-II levels.

NOTES

DO YOUR HOMEWORK...

EVALUATING
YOUR PRODUCT

In the course of considering the purchase of a $500 (retail value) rifle, it would be very easy for the reader to just jump ahead to the TEK-1 Discount Table. He could look down the 30 percent column to the line matching up with 10-12 CSD points and conclude that the "secret" of TEK lies in buying this particular gun at 60 percent of market, or $300. But were he then to go out and offer the gun at $500, he would have missed the TEK system's value altogether. Read on.

6. THE CSD RATING

Take a minute to study the CSD Rating Table (Shown Below). Each column represents one of the three CSD factors: Condition, Scarcity and Demand. Each of these factors is shown with rating levels numbered 0 to 5. In each case, "0" ratings are the least desirable and "5" ratings are the most desirable. The idea is to compare the gun you are considering against these standards and to assign a rating for each category. Add the three numbers together and you have your CSD Rating. You'll accept or reject the trade based on the pre-set level in your own profile.

CSD TABLE

PTS	CONDITION	SCARCITY	DEMAND
5	New or As New	Extremely Rare Artificially Scare	Immediate; booked order Identified positive customer
4	Excellent	Hard To Find	Less than 30 days
3	Very Good	Uncommon	30-45 days
2	Good	Out of Production, But Still Common	45-60 days
1	Fair	Recently Discontinued	60-90 days
0	Poor	Current production	over 90 days

7. CONDITION

Learning to speak "Conditionish" is essential.

> *Ring-a-ling-a-ling.*
> *"Hello, this is George."*
> *"Hi. My name's Bob (or Joe or Jim) and I've got a gun to sell."*
> *"Great. What is it?"*
> *"It's a Remington (or Winchester or Marlin) 742 in .30-06 with a Redfield*
> *(or Tasco or Leupold) scope on it."*

Let's stop the tape on this scene for just a minute. Over the years, I've had this kind of opening conversation many hundreds of times with potential sellers, and it continually amazes me that while, up to this point, we've been speaking in English, we are about to switch over to something I call "Conditionish." "Conditionish" is a gun trading language used between sellers and buyers, but unlike most languages, with Conditionish, the same word can mean different things to each of the parties. Back to the phone . . .

> *"OK, what shape is it in?"*
> *"Oh, it's in great shape. Hardly been used at all. Carried it a lot, but*
> *I haven't shot it much. My Dad got it when he started hunting."*

Stop again. So what shape is this family heirloom really in? Unfortunately, the potential seller is speaking "Conditionish." As you'll see from the "possible translation" table below, "Conditionish" words can be widely interpreted:

WHAT THE SELLER SAYS:	**COULD MEAN:**
"Great shape"	*Considering what it's been through.*
"Good shape"	*It works.*
"Normal wear and tear"	*Scratches and dings all over.*
"Has a lot of character"	*You can still see where Uncle Joe dropped it off that cliff 20 years ago.*
"Stock has been repaired"	*The crack is 1/2" wide and covered with extra glue.*
"Could use a good cleaning"	*You can't see daylight through the bore.*
"Has a nice patina"	*It's rusty all over.*
"The action is a little finicky"	*It functions properly about 20 percent of the time.*

And so on.

Obviously, you want to spend as little time as possible slogging through the mud of "Conditionish," so for all of our evaluations, we'll use a specific set of condition standards developed by the National Rifle Association many years ago. These are shown in the two tables below: separate lists for modern and antique guns because this will better reflect what you are apt to find. These condition grades are universally accepted in gun trading circles and will take most of the interpretation out of describing condition. When you talk to a buyer or seller about a particular gun's condition, be clear that you are using these criteria . . . for example, "NRA Good" rather than "good" condition.

Now, of course, if the other party isn't familiar with these standards, it won't help the conversation much. You'll soon find yourself asking a series of questions during that phone call that can't be misinterpreted. You'll also come to rely only on a visual inspection to establish condition for yourself. And learn not to be disappointed, or at least not to show it, when what you were promised isn't what walks through the door. "Flintlocks" will almost always turn out to be caplocks, "original finish" will often be "original refinish," and a "1901 Springfield" will likely turn out to be something else (more on that one later).

NRA CONDITION STANDARDS FOR ANTIQUE FIREARMS

Factory New – 100 percent original parts and finish, both inside and out. Perfect in every detail. Unfired except by the factory or arsenal.

Excellent – All parts original, at least 80 percent original finish. All markings sharp, with unblemished wood. Bore bright and unpitted.

Fine – All parts original, with at least 30 percent original finish. All markings sharp, with small handling marks on wood. Bore in good condition.

Very Good – All parts original, with less than 30 percent original finish. Markings are clearly legible. Metal smooth, all edges sharp. Wood may have minor scratches and dings. Bore condition is generally not considered in rating an antique arm.

Good – Some minor parts may be replacements. Metal surfaces smooth or lightly pitted in places, possibly cleaned or re-blued, major markings are clear, wood may have been refinished or have minor repairs. Good mechanical function.

Fair – Some major parts may be replacements, some minor parts may be missing. Metal may be rusted or lightly pitted all over, may be cleaned or re-blued, some edges may not be sharp, major markings at least partly legible, wood shows heavy wear or repair, some cracks may still be present. Mechanical condition is either operational or readily repairable.

Poor – Major and minor parts have been replaced or are needed. Metal is heavily pitted, wood badly worn or broken, markings essentially illegible or completely gone. Doesn't function mechanically. (This condition is referred to later in the text as a "parts" gun.)

NRA CONDITION STANDARDS
FOR MODERN FIREARMS

New – Not previously sold at retail; in same condition as currently produced by the factory.

New, Discontinued – Same as above, but no longer in production.

Perfect – Previously sold at retail, but in "New" condition is every respect.

Excellent – In new condition, used only slightly. No marring of wood or metal, perfect bluing except at sharp edges.

Very Good – In perfect working condition. No noticeable wear on working surfaces, no rust, corrosion or pitting, only very minor surface blemishes.

Good – In safe working condition. Minor wear on working surfaces, all original parts, any finish defects are cosmetic only.

Fair – In safe working condition. Heavy wear, minor replacement parts present or needed, pitting which does not interfere with safe operation, should be free of rust and corrosion, but may show heavy cleaning.

Poor – Not functioning safely or possibly not at all. Heavily worn or corroded, may be in need of major parts or repairs to become safely operational. (This is generally referred to in the text as a "parts" gun.)

Now, while these NRA tables enable us to describe a gun's condition with consistency and clarity, we are still faced with the task of determining exactly what that condition is. For example, is the metal finish original? What about the stock? Has it been repaired? Replaced? How about the sights? Is that buttpad original? And the barrel length?

All of these questions may at first seem a little intimidating, but I think you'll find this is one of the fun parts of the game . . . the evaluation. Let's go through the process point by point.

8. IDENTIFICATION

The first and most important step in our evaluation is to accurately identify the make, model and caliber/gauge of the firearm in hand. Only when you know exactly what you are looking at will you be able to determine whether or not it is in original condition.

For most arms built since the early 1900s, the manufacturer's name is stamped on the receiver or barrel, along with some form of cartridge information, and often a model designation and a serial number. Since the '60s, many American-made guns have also carried a short editorial on safe gun handling, along with an offer of a free owner's manual. So given the manufacturer and the model designation on the arm, the basic identification task is greatly simplified.

More detailed model information, based on barrel length, stock configuration, etc, can usually be had by a quick check of one of the general references listed in this book's bibliography. Also, make it a point to get a copy of every manufacturer's catalog for every year you can. The Internet is fine for current offerings, but there

The Opti-Visor is virtually indispensable to the gun trader. It's available in several magnifications and leaves both hands free to move the gun for a better view. CREDIT: BROWNELLS

is no substitute for an older manufacturer's catalog; not even the best reference manuals. It shows details not included anywhere else, and is invaluable for determining dates of manufacture. Order the catalogs, organize them by year or by manufacturer, put them in a box and keep them until you need them.

Never discard an old gun catalog! And keep you eyes open for original or reproductions of very early catalogs. A number of these are being reprinted just for the collector trade. You may also find them at flea markets, household clean-outs, etc.

At the other end of the spectrum, there are the very early – antique – guns of the 1700s and 1800s. Very often these carry no markings at all, and must be identified from references or by "attribution." Some will be marked in a foreign language, or indicate a place now known by some other name. Positive identification is much harder and therefore much more important to the process.

Sometimes the best way to begin is to go through references comparing the piece in hand to the pictures. But the best source is "someone who already knows," as in the situation I had some years ago involving a small .22 short revolver. It looked very much like a Smith and Wesson, but was unmarked. Knowing that S&W always marked their pieces, I was paging through a thick pistol reference when a customer came along and named it a Manhattan Firearms first model. Seems that he was a fan of early small-frame pistols and had several Manhattans in his collection. So if you have access to one or more of these "live references manuals," cultivate the friendship.

For better or worse, you'll find most of your purchase opportunities lie between these two extremes. In short order, you will acquire the ability to make a basic identification of most guns at a glance, based on general contours. Examples here would be the Winchester 1895, the US Krag, the Browning A-5 and the Colt 1911. Many European arms, particularly military guns, such as the Italian Carcano, the Swiss Vetterli, the British Enfield series, the Russian Mosin-Nagant and the French Lebel, also have distinctive profiles.

You'll learn, from continually paging through your references, to recall having seen "that gun" someplace in the Colt book, or in Flayderman's, or wherever the case may be.

Once you know the make and model, either from experience or from research, you may find that some questions still remain about the cartridge and the chambering. That means you will have to become familiar with the cartridge designations of makers both here and abroad. Modern arms are much easier to handle, primarily because the maker is afraid the user will try to stuff the wrong ammo into the gun. In earlier days, little marking was needed because "everybody knew that particular Winchester was only made in .44-40," and the generally accepted maxim was that if you didn't know what you were doing, you should leave the gun alone.

MAKER OR MANUFACTURER

Today, there are only a relative handful of firearms manufacturers worldwide, but that was not the case prior to mass marketing, rapid transportation and a mobile population. From the early 1800s until the early 1900s, small gunmakers could be found all across the eastern portions of this country, and in most of the small cities and towns in Europe. Some produced original work, some essentially copied designs developed by others. Many used proven designs and added features of their own creation. ("It looks like a Smith, but they never used a trigger like that.")

Most of these makers put identifying markings on their work, either as an actual name or as a trademark. The names were usually in the maker's native language, but often guns were ordered with the re-seller's name shown. You'll see reference to "hardware store" guns – generally inexpensive single- and double-barrel shotguns, frequently made in Belgium, sometimes in England, marked with the name or brand of the hardware distributor who ordered them. Thus you find the "bumblebee" logo, "Jackson and Sons, Phila. Pa," "VLD" (Von Lenkirk and Detmold, NYC), etc.

Sometimes, the names used were an obvious attempt to cash in on a better-known and higher quality competitor's successes. These included Belgian doubles bearing the sound-alike names of Parkhurst Bros. (Parker Brothers), W Scott (W & C Scott), Moore (there were numerous Moore doubles, all good, and all British made), and on and on.

In countries like Austria and Germany, where the guild system was in use, guns built by apprentices were generally put up for sale without any maker's markings at all. (Apprentices, by guild rule, had not yet earned the right to mark their products.) These guns can only be attributed based on style, features, etc. Confusing as this may seem, you'll learn to sort it all out as you look at guns and study your references.

MODEL

Once the manufacturer has been identified, the model in hand becomes the next item to be addressed. Model can mean at least three different things, depending on the maker. When a current maker uses the term, he means that each copy of the model will be the same as every other copy of the model. In other words, every Remington 870 5929 will be the same as every other 5929.

Contrast this with the early Winchester 1894 rifles and carbines. The factory allowed a customer to order from a wide range of options, including such things as barrel length and contour, buttplate shape, sights, magazine length, finish, checkering, engraving, etc. In fact, collectors today eagerly seek these variations, particularly when a gun is discovered to have several infrequently ordered options.

And finally, consider the custom maker. In many cases, this individual used the same basic action for his guns, but essentially tailor-made each gun to the fit and fancy of the customer who ordered it.

So how do we identify the model of the gun in hand? Again, this is often marked on the firearm itself. Beyond the "special order" problems noted above, model problems pop up in a number of other cases, as well. First, there is the "Sears Roebuck" syndrome, in which a manufacturer such as Winchester or High Standard builds a special version of their mainline model for a high-volume re-seller, like Sears, Western Auto, Montgomery Ward, etc. These specials are essentially refeatured to prevent direct comparisons.

Refeaturing might mean slightly different sights, a different checkering pattern, an engine-turning pattern on the bolt or shell carrier, a different buttplate or pad, etc. In most cases, these changes reduced the cost of the gun slightly without really changing it, enabling the seller to charge slightly less for essentially the same gun being sold as the standard model at the local hardware store. On these special guns, the manufacturer never used the same model numbers as he used on the originals, and most weren't even close. Sears model numbers are a tale unto themselves. There may be a pattern to them, but in my opinion, the pattern is obvious only to its inventor, and extensive cross-reference lists have been created to assist in sorting them out.

Another problem you will find involves "enhancements" (not always for the best) over the life of a model. The Remington 12 becomes the 12-A, Winchester's 62 becomes the 62-A, and so forth. The difficulty arises in that the manufacturers sometimes did not make the model switchover all at once. So we see early parts shipped on guns marked with a later-model number. This made complete sense for the maker, since he was using up parts on hand and because the model-number changes were often cosmetic or semi-cosmetic, they had no actual effect on the working of the gun. These partly-early/partly-late guns are generically referred to as "transitional" models.

One firm in particular that does seem to have made model modifications all at once is Smith & Wesson. Their practice is to identify engineer changes within models by the markings on the gun itself. These will be encountered, for example, as a model 19K-1, 19K-2, etc. See Roy Jinks' *History of Smith and Wesson* (Beinfeld Publishing) for a full treatment of these changes.

Many consider the toughest model challenge to be the manufacture that did not use grade markings, but essentially sold each grade as a different model. Were we to ask such a manufacturer of yesterday about this practice, he would probably look at us disdainfully and reply, perhaps with a sniff, "the differences among the arms we produce are quite obvious to our customers."

What this really meant was that they made only one model of the gun, but would customize it according to the buyer's wishes. Features such as cartridge or gauge, barrel shape and length, chokes, sights, shape and length of stock, stock grip and forearm size, checkering patterns, fanciness of wood and degree of embellishment (inlays, engraving and plating), could all be specified when the gun was ordered. Within limits, every gun was a custom piece, and this is one of the collector's grails . . . the infrequently ordered, special-order feature.

If you compared a "plain" Winchester 1894 to a "super-fancy" Winchester 1894, you would see the same markings on both, and the pricing difference would be based on the extras. This is a different case from that of the Ithaca and Lefever Hammerless guns, where the basic model distinction was that of side-lock or box-lock. However, each of these was made in many grades, and each grade carries a separate pricing structure. Markings were basically the same for all grades.

Of course, and we will return to this point several more times, we are assuming in our identification process that everything we are looking at is presently as it was when it left the factory or armory. Post-production changes are a real identification headache for the gun trader. I call it the "collar and cuffs" problem. When they don't match, a little voice starts talking to you. Many times the temptation is to tell the voice, as Archie Bunker would say, to "stifle." But listen to that voice. Figure out what it is talking about, and if you can't, pass on the piece.

My first lesson on this involved a Savage Model 99. Maybe it's just me, but I run into a lot a difficulty properly identifying variations of the 99, even with the use of good references. The metal was beautiful, but the stock had appreciable wear, including a nick right at the edge of the metal. I knew, even then, that since the mark didn't continue onto the metal, something had been fixed. I concluded that the metal had been refinished, even though it looked factory original. But I still could not come up with a variation ID. Nowhere could I find that the style of stock had been mated to the feature, style and caliber combination in hand.

Finally I contacted Savage and learned that, when the gun left their Utica, NY, plant, it had a completely different stock! Why had the owner changed it? And why had the gun been refinished? No one can say for sure, but I now believe that perhaps the original stock had been damaged beyond repair when the gun was nearly new, and the owner had installed a used stock as a replacement. Or perhaps this was a replacement for a damaged rifle, and the new owner liked the way his old stock fit, so he switched stocks.

Today I know that Savage marked the serial number of the rifle on the original wood. That would have been a useful piece of information to have back then. Would it have made a difference? Only in being able to explain to a customer why the collar didn't match the cuffs.

PROOF MARKS

Proof marks are important to you as a gun trader, so you will want to put a good reference in your library, such as *The Standard Directory of Proof Marks* by Gerhard Wirnsberger, translated by R. A. Steindler. There are other books around on the subject, but this one seems quite complete.

When a firearm is proofed, or in proper English, proven, the barrel is subjected to a deliberate overcharge, generating from two to three times the pressure levels anticipated in actual use. If it survives intact, it has "passed proof" and moves forward in the manufacturing process. If it fails, it moves to the scrap pile.

Today, American makers proof-test their guns at the factory or arsenal, and most do mark them with a specific stamp. But that stamp tells us little other than that the gun was proofed.

With European makers, however, the story is altogether different. There, the proof testing is done at one of several government proof houses, and barrels passing proof are marked according to the existent "law of proof" in that country. When one first encounters a European double shotgun, for example, it is easy to be confused by the array of proof markings on the barrels and receiver. You, however, will soon learn to read the story written there–everything from where and when the proofing was done, to what proof load was used.

For starters, the marks will indicate the country of manufacture of the barrel, and in some cases, the receiver. Each country uses its own series of marks, and they are readily distinguished from one another. When you find a shotgun with barrels marked "Fine London Twist," it would be easy conclude that the arm is English. Dismount the barrels and you may well find the ELG and peron markings used by Belgium. Why the Fine London Twist label? Perhaps it sold better.

Further, you will be able in many cases to establish a time period in which the gun was built. Let's say that the gun shows mark "A," which was first used in 1891, and a second mark, "B," first used in 1898, but does not show mark "C," which first appeared in 1912. You can conclude that the gun was made between 1898 and 1912. If you are trying to decide whether the gun was built by Company A or by Company B, and you know that Company B bought out Company A in 1913, you now have evidence that the gun was built by Company A. Sometimes this information is important in determining the value of the gun in hand; other times it just tells you more about the piece.

Most European shotguns will carry, as a part of the proof marks, the gauge and chamber length of the gun. This eliminates the possibility of an error in doing your own measurements. Another very important mark will be the Nitro proof stamp, showing whether the gun was tested with black or smokeless powder. This is useful information all by itself, but it can also help determine whether the barrels are of fluid steel or Damascus (twist) construction. While some fluid steel guns were proofed with black powder, the reverse will not be true. If you see black powder proofs on barrels, you would do well to decide that the barrels are not fluid steel, even if you are unable to detect the usual Damascus pattern. Since some fluid steel barrels carried a Damascus pattern finish, considered more attractive at the time, the proof is a more reliable indicator of strength.

Realize also that some handguns and rifles were made in black and smokeless versions, with the receiver being strengthened in the latter case. Examples might include small pocket revolvers, which were intended for .22 black-powder shorts only (smokeless shorts would strain them greatly), and rifles built for cartridges which began life as black-powder loads, but which are currently loaded with smokeless. The Remington rolling block is an example of this.

In looking over the proof markings on a gun, the first thing we see is that every barrel proofed in a given country is stamped in the same way, using the proof marks of the day. On double guns, the separate markings indicate that each barrel was tested independently. Remember that all of this testing was/is done prior to assembly. Every country uses, at a minimum, a "definitive proof" mark indicating that proof was passed. Most also indicate the cartridge used, the load used, whether black or smokeless powder was used, the place of proofing, if there's more than one proof house, and often the date of proof. So by looking at this group of markings, we can tell that the gun is designed to be safe to fire with certain loads. But the proof marks have a far greater value to us than simply that. They can be of enormous aid in identifying, aging and placing guns that are otherwise unmarked with that information.

Case in point. A lady once brought me, for sale, three guns that had belonged to her late husband. They were described in our phone conversation as "a flintlock from the Revolution, a Civil War musket, and a Springfield Model 1901."

We'll talk about the last two later, but first let's look at the gun from the Revolution. When she arrived, she said she knew the gun was from that time period because her departed husband had told her it was, and because a date of "1776" was clearly marked on the lockplate.

Remember the little voice we talked about earlier? Always listen to it, but especially so in the case of an arm with a potential historical aspect to it. (A Colt revolver commands a certain price, but document it as having been issued to someone in Custer's command at Little Bighorn, and watch the price zoom.) This was definitely a flintlock, and it was marked 1776, so what was the voice concerned about? It was saying, "If this piece is genuine, it will be expensive, so be sure it is genuine."

There were basically two types of muskets used by the Continentals (the good guys) in the American Revolution. The first was the musket made in the colonies, or in "the United States" after the shooting started, either under contract for the new government or supplied by individual soldiers from their own resources. This first type is, of course, the most sought-after because of the patriotic aspect.

The second type, and by far the more numerous, consisted of the assorted arms captured or confiscated by the colonies when hostilities erupted, or imported from sympathetic countries by blockade runners. Most of the captured/confiscated pieces were of British manufacture, so it would not have been at all uncommon for American troops to be carrying such guns. Inspection of the gun presented by the lady in our story showed it to be of an English pattern, and definitely a flintlock. So far, so good. The dating, 1776, was quite clear, even though the area around it was not smooth. Again, so far so good.

I've developed the habit, over the years, of inspecting any gun of this type with a magnifying glass. I usually use the Opti-Visor, which is basically a head-band-mounted jeweler's loupe. Using this does two things: It lets me look closely for anything my tired eyes might have missed, and it gives me time to think, do my calculations, and be ready to make an offer or pass when I finish the inspection.

In this case, the loupe made me aware that the 1776 dating was not the only mark on the gun. The date was, in fact, on top of another stamp (the un-smooth area), one that was much older and that was well worn. By looking closely at this second stamp and then consulting a reference, I learned that the proof mark was indeed British, but one that had not been used prior to 1831. Clearly the 1776 stamp was added after 1831. Hostilities with Britain, at least the open ones, had long since ceased before the gun was made.

Why the fictitious date? I can only imagine that someone, perhaps at the time of the first centennial of the Revolutionary War, in 1876, stamped it as part of a celebration somewhere. The work, while clean, was too obvious to have been intentionally fraudulent. Needless to say, the lady was totally unreceptive to the idea that her husband might have been wrong, and left less than happy.

Lastly, proof marks also can indicate, beyond the powder type or weight used in proofing, the actual cartridge for which the arm was intended. This can be particularly important in the case of guns not otherwise definitively marked . . . and many of the older ones aren't. Reading the proofs is much faster than making a chamber cast, and provides more accurate data.

CARTRIDGE

At this point, you know the country of origin, the manufacturer and probably the model of the gun in hand. All that's left is to determine the cartridge.

Perhaps you find the cartridge designated in the proofs, or maybe the model was only made for one cartridge. Either of these makes thing easier. Or you may find a cartridge designation marked on the gun itself. Generally, this will be conclusive, but not always, so let's look briefly at cartridge nomenclature.

European makers use a very simple system for cartridge naming . . . not glamorous, just simple. The two critical measurements (in millimeters) of bore diameter and case length are combined, giving us the 7.62 x 51, the 7.92 x 57, 9 x 21, etc. As I said: simple, not glamorous. Where needed, additional letters are used to address rimmed and rimless versions, differences within a group of similar rounds, etc. The approach makes misidentification unlikely.

American makers, on the other hand, and to some extent our British cousins, have taken the creative approach to cartridge nomenclature–one geared to marketing rather than to ready identification. We use two basic types of nomenclature, and since both have a great deal of flexibility, confusion can result.

The first of these is the "load or use" group, in which the loading, the maker, and the gun for which it is intended are used singly or together to form a designation, as in the .30/30, where the first ".30" indicates the caliber (actually .308), and the second "30" represents the number of grains of black powder in the original loading (even though we use smokeless powder today). Similar examples would be the .30/06 (.30 caliber, developed for the military in 1906), the .30/40 Krag (same idea as the .30/30, but for use in the U.S. Krag rifle), and so on.

The second type is the proprietary name group. The only rule here is that there are no rules, so we wind up with the .30 WCF (Winchester Center Fire, also known as the .30/30), the .45 ACP (Automatic Colt Pistol), the .264 Winchester, the .280 Remington and the .240 Weatherby. There are also the re-namings that happen for safety or marketing reasons. Remington's original 7mm Express round lasted only one year before being renamed the .280 Remington, reducing the chances it would be confused with the 7 Mauser, the 7 Magnum, etc. Remington's .244 was running way behind in its race against the Winchester .243, so it was renamed the 6mm Remington. In this case, the round remained the same, but Remington changed the twist in the barrels of their 6mm guns to better handle the bullet. Today, a rifle actually marked ".244 Remington" can often bring a premium.

There is no system here, so there is no way to "figure it out." One simply studies and remembers. To the beginner, cartridge designations may seem daunting, but you'll get the hang of it in very short order. Your reference library should contain one of the major cartridge guides such as *The Cartridge Guide* (by Ian Hogg, Stackpole Books) or *Cartridges of the World* (Frank Barnes, Krause Publications). As gun traders, we care about this because it assists in identification and because unusual chamberings can have a dramatic effect on firearms value.

But finally, if all else fails, we may be able to determine the intended cartridge for our firearm only by making a cast of the chamber. This may sound messy and/or potentially damaging to the gun, but such is not the case. Brownells sells a solder-like material called Cerrosafe designed especially for casting purposes, which melts at a low temperature and will not harm the gun in any way. It adheres to almost nothing and solidifies in moments, so it isn't at all messy.

There are a couple of tips to remember, however, when using the material. First, it is hot, so handle it carefully. Warm the chamber a little before pouring to slightly retard the speed of solidification. Learn to pour the cast in one steady motion, rather than in two or three passes. Also, learn to pour neither too little nor too much metal into the chamber. Too little will not give a sufficient cast for measuring. Too much will cause overflow into extractor notches, etc., which can make removal of the cast more difficult. Overflow won't damage anything, but may require melting the cast to remove it, then starting over with a fresh pour.

When you plug the bore, use a small wad of cleaning patch and tamp it firmly in the bore. Place it so that at least an inch of bore is also cast, as this will allow an accurate measurement of that dimension, too. Be sure to remove that plug when the cast has been completed! Finally, never discard a cast. Simply toss it back into the melting pot for re-use. The stuff seems to last forever. (See the Appendix for additional chamber-casting instructions.)

CHAMBER LENGTH

Most chambers for metallic cartridges come in only one length, with no long or short versions. Some, however, like the .22 rimfire, the .38 S&W and the .45/XX series, can accommodate several lengths of cases, depending on what the manufacturer had in mind. Assuming the standard markings are not present, and also that no cast has been made of the chamber, one can sometimes use the "try-for-fit" technique as a starter. Metallic rounds of this varying length type will usually be rimmed, so we need "try" only the case itself. If at all possible, use an unfired, empty case. A case fired in another chamber may expand and be oversized for your chamber, giving the false indication that it is not the correct cartridge.

(**Note:** if you are quite sure you know the correct cartridge for the gun in hand, but a case or dummy round won't chamber properly, check to be sure that a cartridge case hasn't been broken off in the chamber. You'd be surprised how easy it is to miss a broken "front end" with a bore light unless you are actually looking for it. If a section is still there, remove it with chamber-casting material. The Appendix provides detailed instructions.)

Obviously, it could be very dangerous to use live ammunition with the "try-for-fit" method, so always use a fired case or a dummy round. See if the case fits flush with the mouth of the chamber. If it will not go flush, and assuming the chamber and rim recess are completely clean, the chamber may be too short or too narrow for the cartridge. The flip side of this, of course, is that if the dummy round drops right in, but projects from the front of a revolver cylinder, impeding the cylinder's rotation, you have a strong indication that the chamber is for a shorter version of whatever you are trying.

If the case does seem to fit properly, run the action through several cycles, again with dummy rounds. If everything works properly, you have identified a possible candidate for "correct cartridge," but you still don't know for sure what you have. The bore diameter may shorten the list further, but only a chamber cast will tell you for sure. Many smiths and gun traders simply go directly to the chamber casting option when the gun is unmarked, knowing from experience that it's where they are going to wind up in the end.

Incidentally, if you are going to use dummy cartridges for function testing and for preliminary chambering identification, be sure that your dummies really are inert! I once received, from a most reputable supplier, a box of .30 Carbine dummies that were not inert. They were, in fact, completely and totally "ert." The manufacturer discovered the error before I got around to using them, and following a somewhat frantic call from the supplier, we got everything straightened out. The lesson here is not to rely on the box label or on the color of the rounds. Centerfire dummy rounds must always have an empty primer pocket. On rimfire dummies, put one in a rifle and safely try it as though it were the real thing before assuming it is a dummy.

"Try-for-fit" can be helpful for metallic cartridges because the case does not change length (other than stretching slightly) when the round is fired, and so this technique is applicable to most rifles and pistols. Shotguns are another story, though.

On a shotgun shell, a small front section of the body is rolled over, or folded over, to prevent the shot from falling out before firing. When the round is fired, the "crimped" portion of the shell has to unfold and straighten to get out of the way of the shot. This means that there must be room in the chamber for the unfolding, lest the crimp interfere (as would a bore obstruction) with the forward progress of the load. Consequently, an unfired shotgun shell will always be shorter than the chamber for which it was intended. For that reason, "try-for-fit" may give false and potentially dangerous feedback. An unfired 3″ magnum 12-gauge load will almost always drop cleanly into a 2 1/2″ or 2 3/4″ chamber. Firing them there, however, is an invitations to disaster.

With most shotguns made after 1950, the barrel will be clearly marked with the chamber length, or with the maximum shell length

Chamber length gauges are a "must-have" for the gun trader who is not limiting himself to factory-marked guns. They can be used for measuring factory work, and also for detecting non-factory alterations. CREDIT: BROWNELLS

to be used. Prior to this time, and especially prior to World War II, U.S. chamber lengths were pretty well standardized at 2 5/8″ (2 9/16″ in 16 gauge). Because only one shell length was generally available, there was no need to indicate what length to use. Everybody "just knew." European chambers ran approximately 2 1/2″ in length or the metric equivalent. This could be discerned, usually, from the proof markings. (See the Appendix for more details on chamber length.)

Unless the arm is clearly marked, you must measure . . . don't guess. The only acceptable way to measure a shotgun's chamber length, other than casting, is by use of a chamber-length gauge. You cannot be a serious shotgun gun trader without a set of these, unless you deal only in marked guns. Your bore gauge may tell you the gun is a 12 ga., but if the 12-gauge chamber gauge won't fit in the chamber, something's wrong somewhere. If you've already narrowed the cartridge down to a small number of possibilities, try a bore gauge. It may, by elimination, give you the answer.

If that fails, measure the bore with a micrometer. Be sure to measure groove to groove for a true reading, and recall that some cartridge names are misleading, as in the .38 Special, which has a bore diameter of .357, and the .303 British, which uses a .311 diameter bullet.

9. ORIGINALITY

When the gun trader discusses condition, he is always implying "original condition." That is, he is observing how closely the gun conforms to its factory-new or arsenal-fresh condition. Very clearly, in order to understand how the gun left the plant, we must know exactly what gun we are looking at. You have to know that what you have is a Parker Brothers Trojan-grade double before you can determine whether or not the barrel length is correct, or whether the buttstock was shortened. So the very first order of business is to identify the piece. Having said that, you can rest assured that every gun trader, admit it or not, has misidentified a piece or two along the way, and then concluded that it was an altered "something-else." Nonetheless, we learn from our mistakes, hopefully, and focus first on proper identification.

With a positive ID in hand, our next task is to determine whether the features of the gun have remained the same since its creation. We're looking here at the features themselves, not at the condition of those features . . . that will come next. It is very easy to try to "take in" a potential purchase all at once. We sweep from end to end, looking at every detail and sometimes not noticing something big.

I recall not long ago looking over a nice Sharps rifle, examining the checkering and the muzzle and the bore very carefully, then suddenly clicking on the fact that this was a percussion gun converted to metallic-cartridge use. That should have been about the first thing I saw. My only defense is that I had seen three other Sharps, all percussion, in the previous couple of days, and apparently just blanked out on the conversion option.

As you gain gun trading experience, you'll start to find yourself rolling the various evaluation steps together and sort of doing them all at once, but when you do, stop and regroup. It's very easy to miss something if you don't follow the same methodical approach with every gun.

Start at either end of the gun; doesn't really matter which. Or even start in the middle, with the action, and then go one way or the other. Do it the same way each time. I start at the buttplate and go forward, but that's just how I do it.

One very useful tool is a description sheet, noting each spot on the gun, such as buttplate, comb, grip, muzzle, trigger, etc. List everything that you might find on any gun or create several sheets, one for rifles, and another for shotguns, etc. Note next to each feature whether it is in its original configuration. This technique is also very handy if you are doing research away from the gun, as in "you can take notes, but you can't take the gun with you. Do you homework and give me a call." Include any measurements that would indicate originality, such as barrel length, length of pull, barrel diameter, overall length, etc. Take the time to measure accurately. This can be tough enough at the bench, but it gets worse in poor light and when your hands are shaking. And trust me on this . . . when the measurement could add one or two digits to the price (for example $500 vs. $5,000), you'll notice at least a small tremor.

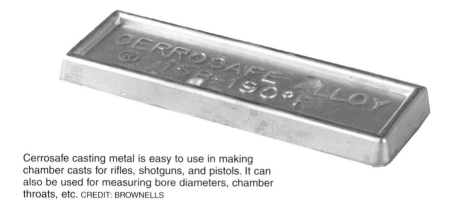

Cerrosafe casting metal is easy to use in making chamber casts for rifles, shotguns, and pistols. It can also be used for measuring bore diameters, chamber throats, etc. CREDIT: BROWNELLS

When you measure, understand where and how to do the job. Knowing how to read your micrometer is important. If you can afford one, it is far easier to read the newer units with digital displays, and you are much less likely to make a mistake in the translation. But it's equally important to know where to measure. Should barrel diameter be checked at the muzzle or just ahead of the receiver? What about the length of pull or barrel length? Some measurements use a standard; some depend on how the factory created the reference. For example, length of pull is always measured from the center of the trigger curve (use the front trigger if there are two) to the center of the side of the buttplate. If there is a cheekpiece in the way, measure on the opposite side of the stock.

Barrel length is also checked in a very specific way, no matter what you might see or hear to the contrary. (By the way, this is the same technique a police agency will use to check for short barrels, so do it their way.) After making sure that the arm is unloaded, close the breech. Carefully insert a straight rod into the bore until it contacts the breech. Mark the rod where it exits the muzzle, withdraw the rod, and measure from the mark to the end that was against the breech. It is just that simple, but you'd be surprised at how many folks don't do it that way. I recall watching a novice scratching his head after trying to do the job with a thin metal tape measure. He carefully slid the tape down the bore until it came to a stop . . . showing him a barrel length of 64″ on a Winchester 1886 rifle. Seems that the tape was curling up in the barrel. Took him a while, but he finally figured out he needed a cleaning rod instead.

METAL AND METAL FINISHES

Another feature to be checked carefully is the type of metal used in the gun, and in the case of shotguns, the type of construction of the barrel(s). It is very easy to assume that a gun frame or receiver is made of steel, but there are other options, each with its own consequences. Early manufacturers often used brass for small pistol and revolver frames, and cast iron for inexpensive receivers. You may also encounter aluminum, titanium, carbon, sheet metal, and probably a few others. The makeup of the frame can be important in determining the variation of the gun, as some makers moved over time from brass to steel, or had a light-weight version of the gun, etc.

When doing this detective work, it is easier to start from where you think you should be, and confirm it, rather than test for everything and discard all the answers but one. If your identification calls for a plated-brass frame, test to confirm that. Test, don't assume. How? In this case, your options would be brass, steel or iron. Eliminate the last two by testing with a small magnet. Then look carefully inside the frame, at the corners, or at any rubbed spots to try to see if the plating has worn away. Tarnished silver can look much like grayed steel on first inspection. Know what you are looking for, and if you find it, great. If you do not find it, and you aren't sure what you did find, move along to the next item and come back here later.

Confirming the makeup of shotgun barrels can be a little tough sometimes, but there some tricks to try. You will encounter a large number of shotguns carrying what are commonly called "Damascus" barrels. They are also sometimes referred to as "Laminated" or "Twist." The barrel maker forged thin bundles of iron wire into a rod, and then joined several rods to make a strip.

The strips were wrapped around a mandrel, heated in a forge, and then the seams were hammer-welded together. This technique produced some remarkably beautiful patterns in the barrel, depending on the number of strips, wires and rods used, varying from simple parallel lines to complex rosettes. In fact, fluid-steel barrels looked so plain in comparison that some firms offered "Damascus Finished" barrels, where the pattern was etched on a fluid-steel barrel.

The problem with Damascus was, and is, that the joinery which made it attractive also made it weak, and in some cases, dangerously so. At the seams where the wires, rods and strips were joined together, it was possible for bubble-like voids to develop. Although they might not be visible on the inner or outer surface of the barrel, these spots made the barrels vulnerable to bursting, especially if subjected to the heavy pressures of smokeless powder.

This was true when the gun was made, and today, in most cases over 100 years later, the danger is even greater. For these reasons, the prices of Damascus and fluid-steel barrels differ significantly. Over time, though, the spirals and lines of a Damascus barrel fade and can sometimes become difficult to see, so if there is any chance the gun you are inspecting doesn't have steel barrels, examine it very carefully with a strong glass under a good light.

Dismount the barrel(s) and look closely at the protected areas, as under the forearm and the water table. Here the pattern will often be more visible, especially right at the edges. If you see pattern, treat the gun as though it is Damascus. Might be the etched pattern, but take no chances. Many of these old guns will have at least some pitting in the bore, and should the pitting occur next to a void, the barrel can be tissue-paper thin at that spot.

Whenever you sell a Damascus barreled gun, it is always prudent to remind the buyer that it isn't safe for use with modern loads. Yes, he should already know that, but I can't tell you how many times I've seen Damascus barrels with fresh powder fouling in them . . . "just low-brass loads." Don't take the chance, and remind you customer not to, either.

There is another method for confirming steel vs. Damascus, involving a little chemistry. You would only be able to do this on a gun you already owned, so its usefulness is a little limited, but it goes like this:

In a "hidden" area, use a little fine crocus cloth to brightly polish a small spot. Then rub the spot with hydrochloric acid. In short order, the pattern, if there is one, will show up at that spot as the acid works at different rates on the softer and harder areas of the twist. There are about four things that can happen with this test, and three of them are not good. And you'll also find that wherever you polish that spot, even right next to the lug, it will stand out very distinctly. So use this test only as a very last resort.

Finally, this is one of those places where your knowledge of proof marks will come in handy, especially on non-U.S. guns. If you find "Nitro" proofs, indicating the barrel was tested with smokeless powder rather than with black powder, you may be sure that the barrel is not Damascus. You may sometimes find that an owner had a set of replacement nitro-proofed barrels installed when smokeless powder arrived. Unless you understand that that was an option, you can easily wind up scratching your head.

Now, for purposes of illustration, let's say that so far we've identified the piece as a double shotgun made in America by the J. Stevens Co. (It says so on the barrels.) We find it to have steel barrels, and they measure exactly 30″ in length, using the technique we just discussed. We can now use a chamber gauge to confirm, as the barrel says, that the gauge and chambers are "12-gauge" and "2 3/4′″". Next, we check the length of pull and get a measurement of 14 1/2″. This falls into the normal range of American stock lengths, which will usually run from 14 1/4″ to about 14 3/4″, so unless we find something definitive about this particular model, we can accept the current length as original. The buttplate is black rubber or hard plastic, and has the Stevens logo on it, and fits well, so that, too, seems OK. So now what?

Now let's move up to the metal and see what we have. You know from your reference book that Stevens usually finished the receivers of their guns with what is called "color-case hardening." In order to increase the durability of the exterior of the receiver, it was heated in a carbon-rich furnace and then cooled. The result is a random pattern that the British sometimes call "brilliant mottle." Like many things in nature, you never know exactly how the colors, which vary from gray to yellow to blue to purple, will mix, but somehow it always turns out.

When newly finished, the effect can run from attractive to stunning. Over time, with exposure to light, the pattern will fade. Handling can dim it more. Two spots that often are spared this fading are the area underneath the top lever and the top of the forearm iron, between the barrel and the forearm wood. You can some-times get a clue as to the brilliance of the original finish by looking carefully at these hideaways. A layer of dust and grease sometimes also protects color-case colors, so if you find a nice old gun in that sort of condition, look underneath.

It is not at all uncommon to find that at some point in the past, a factory color-cased receiver was refinished. Of course, we might have a situation in which it was recolor-cased at the factory, or by a refinisher, but this is an expensive repair, and most smiths are not set up to do it. Because of the high heat involved, the receiver has to be clamped in closely fitted blocks that will keep the piece from warping. Manufacturers have these on hand while the gun is in production, but usually won't recolor-case a gun they no longer make. So when a refinish is called for, the most frequently chosen option is to dump in the hot-blue tank, along with the other parts.

The problem here is that when the metal is polished prior to bluing, it takes on a "greasy" look, almost as if the metal had been smeared a little. Hard to describe the look, but it is one you'll recognize once you see it. Of course, the bluing (oxide) salts do not penetrate the hardened surface well even after the polishing, so the "greasy" appearance carries over with the finished product. The "look" will give away a refinish even when your reference isn't specific as to what the original factory finish would have been.

On occasion, you will find one of the less expensive guns, usually a shotgun, sporting a reddish-colored receiver. The shades may run from purple to dull maroon, but no matter the hue, you are looking at a gun that was originally case-hardened, then redone in a modern hot-blue bath. The cast-iron content in the original metal reacts with the bluing salts to give the red color. This can be counteracted somewhat by adding a compound containing arsenic to the bath, but most smiths don't like to play with arsenic.

Another little trick used to re-do faded color-case is what can be called "colorizing" the surface: a bit of artistry combined with a bit of chemistry. Using a propane torch, the surface is heated while various chemicals are swabbed on in somewhat random patterns. The result certainly looks better than bluing, but it still falls far short of the original. You'll have little trouble identifying colorizing once you've see true color-case hardening.

Some manufacturers are offering their original guns with a "color-case finish," which is not the same as color-case hardening. It is a specialty finish and not the result of surface hardening. Consequently, it does not require the extremes of heat, with the attendant risk of warping. Also, it can be easily repaired by the maker. To the best of my knowledge, no manufacturers are offering this finish on a retro basis, either for their guns or for anyone else's. As with all things, though, this policy could change tomorrow.

It was quite common for makers who color-cased their receivers to also color-case other small parts, including external hammers, top levers, finger levers, and sometimes buttplates, but it was very uncommon to find these small parts colored unless the receiver was also color-cased. Color-cased small parts on a blue receiver may be a clue that the gun has been refinished.

If your reference indicates the rest of the metal was originally blued, and it still looks pretty good, how do you confirm that the finish you can see is original?

When the original finish begins to wear, the bare metal becomes exposed to the atmosphere, and unless the owner is very careful, extremely minute rust spots form. In the presence of normal humidity, these spots will get larger and deeper, forming what are called pits in the metal. These can easily be deeper than they are wide, and they often get a good start before they are noticed.

Cleaning off the rust may stop further damage, but it cannot undo the loss of metal. So when it comes time to refinish, the holes have to be removed by polishing away the surrounding metal, much as you would remove a ding in a piece of wood by sanding down the surrounding surface. To the extent that this polishing is complete, the pit becomes less and less visible. Unfortunately, pits have a habit of occurring in places where it is difficult or unwise to do much polishing, as in stamped or engraved areas. So one way to spot a re-blue is to closely examine (remember that Opti-Visor) the surface for pits which are under the blue finish. In a "normal" pit, the first thing to go is the finish, so if you see blue in the hole, it happened after the pitting occurred. Bingo, a re-blue.

The secret to any blued finish is in the polishing done beforehand. The finishes produced by Smith and Wesson are legendary in the industry, and stories make the rounds of the extensive experience required of polishers before they are allowed to move up to final-pass polishing. The best polishes require the use of a "hard" felt wheel, but the same firmness that makes for a smooth finish also carries with it the danger of the hard edge cutting into the metal. Most refinishers, therefore, use softer felt or muslin wheels. They are much more forgiving and much less likely to cut. They do have one drawback, though: when they go over holes or lettering, they have a tendency, because of their relative softness, to push down into the hole a little, rounding off the sharp edges. Known in the trade as "funneling," this is another sure sign of refinishing.

A readily observable indication of a re-do is the presence of polishing marks. The factory knows how to rotate the parts under the polishing wheel and how to get into all of the corners without leaving any pattern of polishing marks. It requires a variety of different wheel and bob shapes, but the maker has them. On the other hand, most refinishers don't, so they sometimes leave marks behind. Also, you may see that some areas appear more polished that others – again, the result of non-uniform passes under the wheel.

In recent years, makers have brought out a large number of guns in "matte" and "brushed" finishes, rather than in the traditional "gloss" format. Gun marketers tout these finishes as non-reflective, and so less likely to scare game.

There may be some truth to these claims, but factories push this finish for another reason, too. The finish, which is usually achieved by blasting the surface with tiny glass beads, can be done with much less human intervention. Matte finishes are essentially a somewhat uniform overall pattern of pits and scratches, as opposed to the perfectly smooth surface of a gloss finish. The matte surface is non-reflective because the light comes off the various surface marks at many different angles.

Machines matte well, but it takes the human eye to polish. When it comes time to refinish these matte surfaces, some try to achieve the same look by polishing with a coarser medium. This will produce a matte finish, but it just doesn't look like bead-blasting. You'll soon learn to see the difference between the two.

Up to this point, the re-bluing we've been discussing requires the use of special salts in a high-temperature caustic bath. It is essentially the same process whether performed by the manufacturer or by the repair shop, and given a proper polish job, the blued finish itself is the same. There is, however, another re-coloring process known as "cold bluing," in which a chemical is swabbed onto room-temperature or slightly warmed metal to produce a blue-black finish.

The advantage, of course, is ease of application. The down side is that the finish is thin and usually much more fragile than hot blue. A deep, durable and easy-to-apply cold blue is the Holy Grail of gunsmithing.

Cold blue is great when used to touch up screw repairs, pin ends, tiny scratches, etc., but some folks try to re-blue an entire gun with it, and that's where the trouble can start. If cold blue is applied over a good polish job, it may appear uniform, but it will quickly wear off. When applied over the existing surface, frequently without thorough degreasing, the metal often takes on a streaky gray-black look as the chemical bites into the more-exposed metal, and has little or no effect on the areas protected by oil or original blue.

There is also a faint but distinctive odor to cold-blued metal, and this tell-tale aroma should send up a flag. If the metal has been redone, it was redone for a reason. You would be well served to get a bottle of cold blue, find a piece of gun steel, and try to re-blue it. You'll quickly learn to spot the "cold-blue look," and you'll learn to identify the way cold-blued metal smells. When you suspect cold blue, rub the metal gently with your fingers, warming it by friction, and pay attention to what your nose tells you.

Don't confuse this "cold-blue" finish with another metal-darkening technique known a "rust bluing." One of the oldest finishing methods, found on some of the finest guns made, it is also called "controlled rusting," and utilizes the normal processes of nature in a controlled environment.

After proper polishing, the metal is coated in a rusting agent, and then placed in a warm, high-humidity cabinet where it is literally allowed to rust. After a day or so, and before pitting can begin, the rust is gently removed with fine steel wool, leaving behind a blue-black surface. The process is repeated until the finish is as deep and uniform as desired. Then the oxidation process is "killed" or neutralized by washing the rusting agent away and protecting the surface with oil.

This coloring method has the distinct advantage of being compatible with the lead solders used to join the barrels in older double guns. Submerge a soft-soldered double in one of the modern high-temp caustic baths and you stand a good chance of converting that double into two single barrels! You probably won't ever have to worry about someone using rust-bluing to replace factory hot-blue, but if your reference calls for rust blue, shy away if you find anything else. The best way to learn to see the difference is simply to examine several fine old double guns in top condition. The metal has a look and feel that simple cannot be duplicated by other methods.

The military is big on a phosphate-base finish known as parkerizing. Ranging in color from gray to a light gray-green, this finish stands up well to the demands of combat. It is tough and durable, but not particularly attractive. Some phosphate jobs are better done than are others. Compare the finish on an arsenal-original M1 Garand rifle with the parkerizing re-do on some of the M1 Carbines coming back to the U.S. from South Korean surplus dealers. Parkerizing doesn't lend itself well to the small refinisher's setup, so when you see the tell-tale gray-green finish, you are probably looking at something done by a manufacturer or arsenal.

The last applied finish you may encounter, other than paint (which is always a clue), is generally known as "browning." This is another room-temperature process, and it is essentially the same as rust-bluing, except that the rusting agent used produces a brown oxide rather than a black or blue color. It is most often found on early rifles and muskets, and a good practitioner can duplicate the finish rather readily today. When considering arms which would have been originally browned, look carefully for a finish that appears to be "too fine", as it may well be much newer than the gun itself.

Plating is not widely used today, except for occasional presentation pieces, but it was fairly common from the 1850s through WWII, especially on handguns. Early makers often put silver plating on brass or steel frames of their small pocket pistols as an aid in preventing surface discoloration. Nickel, and to a lesser extent chromium, were used in later years to provide a more durable surface, and one less subject to corrosion. The advent of the use of stainless steel in firearms has essentially ended the use of plating.

Metal finishes are time consuming to apply and subject to wearing off, but until recently they were the only way to protect metal from rust, save the military's "wipe every night, used or not" approach. With the introduction of guns made of "stainless" steel, the need for an applied finish was theoretically eliminated, and the marketing appeal of keeping a gun rust-free without constant attention was obvious.

But much to their surprise, some owners found out that "stainless" guns would indeed rust, given enough encouragement. While it takes longer to get started, "stainless" guns, like any other steel, will rust eventually. The confusion occurs because "stainless" can describe any of a variety of steel amalgams of varying hardness, from the super-hard type used for dental and surgical instruments, to the much softer kind used for guns. "Gun stainless" has to be softer so that it can be machined rather than being shaped by grinding, as in the case of scalpels and dental picks.

The big advantage of stainless is that, because it is more resistant to rust, it can be used in damp or corrosive environments and will not begin to rust before you eyes. Take your favorite duck gun to a salt marsh and watch the corrosion happen right in the blind. Or tuck your little hide-out gun into a holster right against your skin in the summertime. Same idea. As a gun trader, look carefully at that stainless gun, especially around the sights and in other hard-to-clean spots. Any darkening of any sort is an indication of poor care or abuse, so be guided accordingly.

Recently, there have been a variety of high-tech finishes introduced, such as baked-on coatings, black chrome, and proprietary finishes. The gun trader needs to concern himself with these only when considering guns of quite recent vintage. All of them have one thing in common: They may be expensive, they may be better than the factory work, but they are still "refinishes." You may add CSD points for demand because of them, but you must also deduct points for originality.

One last thought on finishes . . . they do wear through. It is completely normal to find "tracks" where two parts rub together, as when the locking bolt of a revolver rubs against the outside of the cylinder. They may show themselves as bare metal visible through the blue or as bright marks on a matted finish. This type of mark will always be present except on a brand-new gun, and if you don't see it when you should, suspect a refinish of some sort.

STOCKS

By this point, you have determined whether or not the metal finish is original. Assuming that this answer is acceptable, we now must assess the finish of the wood, and then look at several other points.

I think it's more fun to assess wood than metal, but that's just my opinion. I also think it is easier to make mistakes in assessing wood. With metal, a given "look" can almost always be attributed to a certain process or condition, but with wood, many things look alike.

For starters, let's try to see whether the wood is factory original or a replacement. Sometimes replacements are easy to spot, and in fact they may even be marked. When you see a buttplate marked Bishop or Fajen, you can be quite certain that the stock is one of the excellent replacements sold by those companies when they were in business. They were dimensionally the same as the original when a "100 percent fitted and finished" stock was purchased, but most folks opted for the "semi-inletted" version. This type was about 99 percent correct where metal joined the wood, but the outside shaping and contouring were left up to the customer, along with the sanding, finishing and checkering.

Of course, many restorers used the original buttplate on the replacement stock, so a Savage or other armsmaker's buttplate doesn't always mean the stock itself is original. Conversely, when you know that a manufacturer always used a logo or trademark on their buttplates, and you don't find that logo on your gun, it doesn't necessarily mean that the stock has been replaced. Perhaps it was, or perhaps the prior owner changed only the buttplate itself.

You will occasionally encounter a "home-made" stock, and these are readily identified by their poor contours and fit, and many times by the type of wood used. I once found a Winchester 94 in beautiful condition, except that the buttstock was made from apple wood. The family story was that Grandpa had fallen and broken the stock when the gun was brand new. Believing himself to have skills as a stockmaker, he carved up a local tree trunk to make the replacement. The fit of wood to metal was adequate, but the overall contours were such that one can only hope this was the only restocking job Grandpa ever attempted.

Although makers tried many varieties of stock wood, including gum, ash, myrtle and others, the bulk of sporting arms were stocked in walnut. Many "Kentuckies" will also have stocks of cherry or maple. You'll learn to identify stock woods by color, grain, figure and relative weight. You may, on occasion, pick up the pungent fragrance of walnut when you remove a buttplate or dismount the action. This little extra information will help you reach your conclusion.

A "home-made" stock is not the same as one made by a professional restocker, regardless of where he made it. A proper custom stock of this nature will be a replacement, true, but generally speaking, it will add far more to the value of the arm than it will take away.

Is the stock checkered? If so, is the forearm, whether on a one-piece or two-piece stock, also checkered? Makers didn't checker just the wrist or just the fore-arm. The idea behind checkering is to improve gripping, but checkering large enough and sharp enough to be of any real help will probably tear up your skin under heavy recoil. Most checkering is present primarily as a decorative device. The fineness of the checkering and the ornateness of the pattern generally increase with the quality and grade of the gun. So when only the wrist or only the forearm is checkered, you can almost always conclude you are looking at either a replace-ment or a major refinish (without recheckering).

When you do encounter a gun with only the butt or only the forearm checkered, the question will arise as to which is the original and which is the replace-ment. Since checkering would usually represent a more expensive option, you might easily conclude that the uncheckered component represents the replacement of a damaged original. Perhaps, but sometimes further detective work uncovers another answer. I purchased a Savage 99 (another mysterious 99) that had a factory-checkered wrist and what was obviously a home-style attempt to checker an otherwise plain forearm. Clearly the forearm was a replacement that someone had doctored up . . . except that both the butt and forearm carried the serial number of the gun!

Careful scrutiny disclosed that there was some "dishing" on the forearm, where the surface had been sanded or cut down. The amateur checkering was then applied to this new surface. The only explanation that makes sense seems to be that the original forearm was badly scarred, perhaps in a fall. The owner, perhaps a rel-ative of Grandpa with the apple-wood stocked 94, apparently sanded down the damage, then had a go at checkering it with his pocketknife. This knowledge may not really have that much effect on the price of the gun, but it would help to ease the concerns a customer is bound to have with the apparent mismatch.

Is the checkering on the gun you're holding original? I can only say that checkering cut by the professional stockmaker or by the factory just "looks right." Whether it is "positive" (points stick up) or "negative" (points are pressed in with a hot iron), the design is even and the position on the stock is both centered and square. Factory checkering can be cut using hand-held tools or by a computerized "cutter." Either way, there will be virtually no run-outs in the pattern, where the checkering lines extend past the edge of the pattern. Some stockers use a border to cover run-outs, and that's OK, too. But when you find a pattern that is lopsided, tilted or with lines that are not evenly spaced, beware. The style may be pointed or flat, but it must be uniform.

Closely inspect the mating of wood to metal. Most guns were designed to have a fit in which the wood is tight to the metal and is also flush, or nearly so, with the surface. On some inexpensive modern arms, this closeness is achieved by sharply beveling the edge, but the net result is the same (though less attractive). In no case, ever, was the stock left below the surface of the metal or well above it. In the first case, the metal was unprotected from snags, and in the second, the wood fibers were apt to swell and break off. Too much wood signals a replacement stock, while depressed stock edges indicate overzealous sanding during a refinish. One of the tricky spots to get right during a stock re-do is at a sharp corner of a receiver. Unless the stock and metal are dressed together, great care must be used to avoid a "round-over" on the corners. These are among the most obvious of refinishing flags.

Now look at the color of the wood where it meets the metal. Over time, this wood/metal joint collects all manner of dirt, grease, oil and moisture. It absorbs oil and grease, and frequently darkens significantly. The wood immediately to the rear of the action is especially susceptible to oil staining when the gun is stored vertically in a rack for an extended period. Once the wood becomes oil darkened, it is extremely difficult to get it light again. The rest of the surface may look as new as can be, but these dark edges are a major giveaway. Also, the original edges tend to expand and contract a little, leaving them a bit rough to the touch. As the finish wears there, the roughness will increase.

Check the stock for those nicks and dings that are almost inevitable on a "pre-owned" piece. You'll find two types of damage: The first will be spots where the stock has been banged against something smooth; the wood will be dented, but sound. We call these "compression dings." They are very common and don't necessarily mean the gun was abused, simply that it was handled. If you don't find any of these, look again for evidence that they were removed. The standard technique is to apply moist heat to the ding, causing the wood fibers to swell back into position. When done correctly, this remedy will restore the wood to its original position and make the damage hard to see. Sometimes though, especially with the synthetic finishes, the impact breaks the finish skin and allows the moisture to get underneath. This in turn can cause a whitish area around the spot that is very hard to eliminate without removing the raised finish and replacing it.

The second bit of badness that happens is the impact point where wood is actually gouged out, leaving a hole behind. The moist-heat treatment won't correct this one because there is no wood to decompress, and the damage can only be corrected by filling or by sanding down the adjacent area and refinishing the wood. Large areas are sometimes repaired by inletting wood of similar grain and color.

With hot shellac properly color matched to the stock, it is possible to fill the gouge and create a nice smooth repair, but it is virtually impossible to hide it from a trained eye.

For starters, the color itself will almost never be of exactly the same tone as the stock itself. Secondly, gouges are often quite inconsiderate in that they usually disregard grain lines, making a very obvious mark. This interruption of the natural grain flow grabs the eye like a waving flag, even if the surface finish has been completely restored. I've seen almost unnoticeable repairs of this type on highly figured wood, but on the plainer, straight grained stocks of most guns, they do tend to stand out.

We also need to look for any cracks or checks in the wood, either open or repaired. Cracks are simply spots where the wood fibers have separated all the way through, while checks are surface expansions in the grain. Checks can happen anywhere on the stock surface, but are especially common near the center of highly figured areas. They happen because the wood expands and contracts at different rates over the harder and softer areas of figured wood. Properly seasoned wood coated with a penetrating finish seems to be less susceptible to checking.

Cracks can happen from the natural expansion and contraction of the wood, or they can be caused by accidents. They almost always follow the grain, and small ones can be hard to spot, especially when the surface is not perfectly clean. Unfortunately, small cracks have a way of growing into larger cracks.

Successful prospecting for cracks begins by knowing where they are most likely to be found. Any place where the wood is thin or subject to impact is a likely candidate for a crack. On shotguns, the juncture of wood to metal at the rear of the receiver takes a beating every time the gun is fired. Unless the metal bears evenly on the wood, the force of the recoil is concentrated on a smaller area and this can cause a crack to develop.

The rear end of the trigger guard is another spot to look. On guns with sideplates, recall that the sideplate is firmly fastened to the rest of the action, so when the action recoils, so does the sideplate. Cracks can often be found at the rear of the plate area. Magazine wells also lend themselves to cracks. On forearms, the spot to check is just ahead of the metal at the rear, when the wood, moving backward under recoil (minutely, but still moving) encounters the resistance of the metal in the operating handle or the forearm iron. Forearm tips, especially those made of exotic woods like rosewood or ebony, are prone to cracking, both where they join the stock and along their own grain lines.

In the case of rifles, particularly those subjected to the heavy recoil of powerful cartridges, cracks can develop at the rear of the receiver tang, at the rear of the recoil lug, and at the rear of the magazine well. Any time a heavy cartridge is involved, it's a good idea to remove the barreled action from the stock in order to examine the interior inletting. I've seen rifles that looked good on the outside, but had badly cracked interior webs, usually caused by poor bedding of the recoil lug against the stock. Every time the rifle recoiled, it slammed into the stock.

Cracks and splits caused by accidental impact can happen anywhere on the gun, but the thin areas succumb more readily. Shocks occurring in very cold weather, as when a deer rifle is dropped on the toe of the stock, can cause a clean and complete break with little other visible damage. This can be repaired rather successfully if the broken piece is carefully retained and promptly replaced, but the thin joint line can usually still be seen.

The same break can happen at the edges of the pistol grip, and one of the benefits of a grip cap is that it shields the stock edges from exactly that impact. The sharp edges of the stock, where it meets the metal, are prone to having splinters pop off. Cheekpiece edges can also be easily damaged. It is interesting, however, that as the quality of the stock work increases, the less of this sort of thing you find. I once thought that this was because people who owned fine guns took better care of them. Now I realize that it is primarily due to the care the stock's maker took to slightly, almost minutely, radius every edge, giving fewer opportunities for a direct blow to land. Machines can create a flat surface with crisp edges, but it requires careful handwork to trim the edges into a radius that appears sharp.

Certain areas of the stock are also liable to warp, even if the wood does not split or check. Whenever you have a true tang at the rear of the action extending into the stock, the wood at either side of the tang will be fairly thin. These thin areas frequently warp, moving away from the metal by as much as 1/8″. If they seem springy, it is a clue that they have warped or are likely to. This type of defect is very, very tough to repair.

Another spot that can readily warp, and one in which the warping is harder to spot, is on a rifle's forearm along the barrel channel. This is a double whammy, affecting both the appearance and the accuracy of the gun. Look at the clearance of the wood on either side of the barrel. It should be uniform from end to end. A small amount of clearance is a sign of good workmanship, but uniform clearance is more important. Also look at the forearm from both sides. The top edge should be uniform in relationship to the edge of the barrel. It may or may not be exactly parallel, depending on the design of the stock and the taper of the barrel, but it should definitely be uniform.

If possible, dismount the action from the wood to check further for damage. This can be asking a lot of the seller, but it can also be very revealing. As we mentioned, many times the "web" of wood in the inletted area of the stock will show splitting that is not at all evident on the surface. Another spot to examine, on two-piece stocks, is the bearing area at the front of the buttstock. Cracks here will be at right angles to the grain and are much easier to see. Again, these may or may not be visible on the surface. Always remove the forearm on a double (or single-shot) shotgun and examine the wood for cracks and also for evidence refinishing. If for some reason the owner is reluctant to allow this kind of examination, antici-pate the worst and factor it into your purchase offer.

The final thing we'll check on the stock is the finish itself. Over time, stocks have probably been finished, or refinished, using almost anything you can think of, from paint to bear grease. But the majority started out in life with finishes that fall in the category of oil, varnish, or synthetic.

Remember that we are trying to determine whether the finish is what is should be, not whether it was a good choice on the part of the maker. Synthetic finishes are a fairly recent development, and so should not be present on older guns. These are mostly complex coatings, hard to duplicate outside the factory, and for that reason, about the only one we are apt to encounter in the wrong spot is polyurethane. "Poly-U," as available to the home gun hobbyist, is not quite the same as the urethane-based commercial finishes, and so usually stands out. It is prone to developing a case of "the sags" after application, and also tends to cloud up over time.

Manufacturers often used varnish as a finish, but it needs to be refreshed every so often, so most varnish finishes you see today, if original, will be in need of repair. It is possible to find one that has been carefully protected, but when you see one in tip-top shape, take a second look.

Oil-based finishes are frequently encountered, particularly on the finer guns, where it was carefully rubbed into a fine luster. The advantage of the oil finishes is that they soak into the wood to an extent, whereas the synthetics tend to form a shell over the wood, much like a peanut shell.

The point here is that you'll want to learn to recognize the various finishes used. Most importantly, learn how to spot refinishes. Of course, runs and sags in the surface, regardless of the material, are a giveaway. Manufacturers simply didn't let that kind of thing go out the door. A second obvious pointer is the presence of a "wavy" stock surface, indicating that the wood was hand-sanded before being refinished. Makers used sanding equipment designed to avoid these ripples, but many hobbyists haven't learned the tricks. When you see stock finish, no matter what kind, continuing beyond the wood onto the adjacent metal, you know not only that the wood has been redone, but also that the re-doer was too lazy to remove the wood from the gun first.

And if all else fails, look very closely at the nicks or tiny dings in the wood. If you see finish in these places, it was applied after the nick happened, particularly if the damage is not a compression ding. You'll also often see original dark finish in these "pits," even though the surrounding wood is bright and fresh. If you can pull the wood off the gun, look at the hidden edges. I'm always amazed at how often folks do an outstanding job on refinishing the exterior of a stock, but totally ignore the inside surfaces. The mating of the old and new finish surfaces stands out even to the novice eye.

We have been talking about wood stocks all this time, but most of it applies to any other stock materials, with the exception of finishes. The alternative to wood is the synthetic stock, either today's nylon or carbon designs, or one of the few old "plastic" types. Many years ago, Savage-Stevens used a hollow "Tenite" stock on several of their guns. It was innovative and promised lightness along with increased resistance to weather and wear. But it had a tendency to scratch and, in severe cold conditions, it was apt to crack. After molding, these stocks were simply buffed, and no additional coatings were applied.

This is also the case with modern nylon and carbon matte finishes. There is no external finish to wear through. They are what they are, all the way through. One caution with the Tenite stocks: When you find one, it probably is original to the gun, but many times the original plastic stock was replaced with wood. Consult your reference on these guns and be sure you have plastic where plastic is called for.

THE EFFECT OF REFINISHING ON A GUN'S VALUE

Refinishing a firearm, in full or in part, may or may not have an impact on the value of the gun. The answer depends on the nature and condition of the gun in question, and on the skill of the refinisher.

Assuming that it is done to factory standards, refinishing will generally have a positive or neutral effect on the price of commonly encountered modern arms, where the finish is well worn. By a neutral effect, I mean that the price of the gun may increase by the value of the refinish, but not more than that. A positive effect may be seen on more expensive modern guns when the finish itself is badly worn, but the underlying surfaces are still in good condition. This sometimes happens when a gun rusts, or a stock finish breaks down from exposure to something in the lining of a gun case. Here, the value of the refinished gun will usually be higher than the price of the damaged gun plus the cost of refinishing. The price will usually be less than, and will never exceed, the value of a gun in equivalent original condition.

My guideline for "factory standards" is that the refinish was done by the factory or by a shop using factory materials and techniques. If you can tell the gun has been refinished, it hasn't been done to factory standards, and an amateur refinish will not help the value of the gun.

Refinishing will often have a negative effect on price when we are dealing with an older gun. This is because buyers want the gun as it is, with whatever battle scars it has accumulated over the years. If the arm has deteriorated to the point that it has little value, a full restoration will increase the price you can ask for the gun, but you may or may not come out ahead after deducting the cost of repairs.

Finally, there is a class of arms that should never be refinished: Guns that are specifically connected to an historic event should be left as they are whatever that condition may be. Protecting them from further deterioration is altogether different from refinishing. The most commonly used example of this type of arm is the pistol used by John Wilkes Booth to assassinate Abraham Lincoln. There was a small chip of wood, along with a small screw, missing from the gun when it was taken from Booth at the time of his capture. These defects are important to the piece, and repairing them would be a grave error.

Similarly, almost anything in the "antique" category should be left as is. Resist the urge to "shine her up a little," and practice self control when you encounter someone who has sanded and re-blued a Sharps.

10. SCARCITY

The second component of the CSD table is the scarcity factor. There is sometimes a tendency to roll up scarcity and demand into the same package, but they are distinct items and will exert very separate influences on your purchase decisions.

When we say that a particular gun is scarce, it simply means that there aren't many around. It used to be that scarcity frequently had a local, regional or even national side to it. I can recall when New England and the South were the places "where you find doubles and antiques," while the western states were home to the Winchesters, Colts, etc. sought by collectors. The Internet has had a impact on smoothing out these regional differences to an extent, but they are still a factor, especially at the primary source level. You probably aren't going to find a lot of Colt Peacemakers sitting in closets in Vermont. This "regionality" does, however, still play a strong role in the demand for certain models, as we will discuss in the next section.

A given make or model of firearm could be scarce for a number of reasons. Perhaps only a small number were ever made in the first place. The lady with the 1776 musket, discussed earlier, also told me about her late husband's "1901 Springfield rifle." Of course, my immediate reaction was, "Don't you mean 1903?" "No," she assured me, "I'm looking right at it and it says U.S. Springfield Model 1901." Some quick research told me that there were fewer than 30 of this experimental rifle built, and that the whereabouts of all but a few were well documented. Was it possible that she had one of those remaining few?

When she arrived at the counter, the rifle was cased, almost, it seemed, to prolong the suspense. As I drew the gun from the cover, the distinctive "box-on-the-side" profile of a Krag rifle came into view. "I'm sorry," I said, "but this isn't a Model 1901."

She was having none of it. "Of course it is! It even says so right on the side. Look right there," she exclaimed, pointing to a stamped line of the side of the receiver.

I looked, of course, and found that it read "U.S. Springfield, Model 1896," and then saw, about 6″ to the right, the serial number, 1901. Somehow, she had looked at it, not just once but several times, and just passed right on through the part about 1896. How, I have no idea, but she did.

The lesson to be learned here? When someone tells you they have a great rarity, go forward eagerly, but don't be disappointed when the bubble bursts. There is always a chance that it will pan out, but the odds are all against it.

Particular guns may also be scarce because the design proved unpopular. My favorite example of this is the Winchester Model 1911 shotgun. This gun came onto the market when John Browning's design was selling as the Remington Model 11. The Winchester 1911 was intended to compete without violating the Browning patent, and the result was one of the most forgettable shotgun designs of the 20th century. As one gun writer put it to me in the 1970s, "My father had one that worked perfectly, but every other one I've ever encountered was an absolute lady dog." Today, the Winchester 1911 is considered a fairly scarce gun, and I suspect it is because so many early owners wrapped theirs around the nearest tree.

Sometimes the manufacturer died unexpectedly, or the business folded, and again the result was that only a few guns were ever made. It was not uncommon for the American government, in the early years, to contract with numerous small makers for arms. Some contracts were completed, some were cancelled, and some were only partly filled. Often these contracts were for no more than a few hundred guns. Losses in battle combined with normal wear and tear results in scarcity today. The older the gun, the more chances there has been for things like these to happen. It is normal for them to occur, and when they don't occur, collectors do a dance.

There were also wholesale conversions, particularly with military arms, when new technology became available. Sharps rifles were converted from percussion to metallic cartridge, Springfield muskets went from flintlock to percussion cap, and so on. I sometimes wonder, given that these were government arsenal conversion programs, how any pieces at all escaped the changeover. Occasionally, arsenals retired and destroyed entire armament lines as they became obsolete, but more often these were released to the private sector, both here and abroad.

Sometimes just the opposite happens, providing more specimens than one might expect. Remington produced a large number of Moisin-Nagant rifles under contract for the Russian Czar, but before they could be delivered and paid for, along came the Bolsheviks. Most of the guns still in Remington's possession were released to the American market. They are often encountered, and usually in surprisingly good condition.

Commercial conversions also will be found, such as Winchester's offer to swap Model 1893 pump shotgun actions for the stronger 1897 version. As a more current example, Ruger still offers free conversion of their original revolvers to the safer transfer bar system.

We will also encounter the condition I call "artificial scarcity." Here, the maker produces fewer of a given model than the market wants. Sometimes this is the result of poor planning, and sometimes it is very deliberate. Manufacturers have to guess what the marketplace wants many months in advance, and there are lots of things that can happen after production schedules are locked in. They can cancel quantities, but they can rarely increase them in the short run.

All of this can result in temporary spikes in demand. Although I will usually suggest that production guns be avoided by the gun trader (leave them to the retailer), these spikes can provide an opportunity for the someone who is paying attention to the marketplace. A similar phenomenon exhibits itself when a manufacturer advertises a new model way before it is actually available. They walk a fine line between building demand and frustrating their potential customers. I recall that when the Ruger Redhawk was introduced, initial shipments were very limited. Customers were offering prices nearly twice the suggested retail price in order to latch onto an early arrival.

Presentation pieces are another example of artificial scarcity. In a common example, the ornate guns created for auctioning by Ducks Unlimited, the NRA and similar organizations are truly one-of-a-kind guns, which of course is why folks pay top dollar for them.

Another form of limited production is the commemorative firearm. Back in the 1800s and early 1900s, medals, knives and other items were often issued to mark or remember people, places and events. They were never made in large quantities, they were generally not too expensive to begin with, and since most were also useful items, like knives or screwdrivers, their survival rate into the 1950s was very low.

Prompted perhaps by the emerging "collectibles" market, commemoratives started showing up from Colt and Winchester in the 1960s, most notably in the Winchester 94 series. The idea was, of course, to stimulate sales. They were built to remember everything from WWI battles, to the granting of statehood, to American heroes.

The Winchester issues were made as rifles, as carbines, as sets, in color case, in silver, in gold, with octagon barrels, round barrels, etc., etc. Each commemorative was a Winchester 94, but each was supposed to be slightly special. Even the box was specially marked. In concept, the customer who would normally have purchased one Model 94 might now be tempted to buy several. Other makers dipped their toes in the commemorative water, but Winchester jumped right in.

During much of the commemorative era, from the early 1960s to the early 1980s, prices were also on the rise, pushed by rising interest rates. Of course, this inflation, coupled with the "collectibles" interest, drove up prices for the older commemorative material at a remarkable pace. This was not lost on gun manufacturers. The marketing approach was something like, "Imagine what a gun, built 100 years ago to mark a particular event, would be worth today if it had been kept in the box and just put away! Well, these are the next best things. Each issue is unique, and if you hold onto them, they'll be worth a lot more in the future than they are today. Look at how prices have been jumping for the last ten years."

The whole thing might have worked out better had inflation continued to push prices up, and had the makers not tried to maximize sales. Interestingly, the first two issues were brought out in smaller numbers than the later ones, sold out quickly, and are still in demand today. There is a natural tendency, when production is sold out, to believe that additional production will also sell out. This is only my own observation, but it seems to me that there were sufficient quantities of each issue produced to meet the demand of anyone who wanted one.

The guns were not cheap, there were a lot of variations issued, and most importantly, I believe, the guns held their value, as commemoratives, only while in new-in-the-box condition. As soon as they were fired, the values dropped to those of the Model 94, then in regular production. This standard model was generally considered a hunting firearm, but some of the commemorative issues were brightly plated or carried heavy octagonal barrels. These features limited their utility in the field, so once fired or scratched, their value dropped further.

Finally, inflationary pressures eased off in the late '80s, and the hoped-for price growth didn't materialize. Eventually, these Winchester commemoratives, along with those of other manufacturers, may suffer enough attrition through natural losses to actually become scarce, but I believe that point is well out in the future. There is a market for them today, but scarcity is not the primary focus.

Unlike commemoratives, limited-edition guns are produced by manufacturers with the understanding that only a relatively small number of units will be sold. Consequently, they make sure to price them accordingly. Modern examples of limited editions would be the Browning series–basically re-issues of guns originally made by Winchester's sister company (USRA), which should not be confused with the originals. Probably the best known of the limited-edition guns are the Winchester 1873 and 1876 "1 of 100" and "1 of 1,000" guns. These are among the most sought-after Winchester prizes, and were intended to be so from the start.

The final form of artificial scarcity is that caused by governmental regulation, especially in "grandfathering" situations. When possession of a particular arm is simply prohibited to all, scarcity happens instantaneously and that model is no longer in play in a local or national market.

Grandfathering, which basically allows only some specimens of the gun to be traded, has the same effect as destroying the banned units. Assuming that the same number of people still want one, prices climb. Conversely, as demonstrated by the 2004 sunsetting of the oxymoronic Federal ban on "semi-automatic assault weapons," the reverse result occurs when these grandfathering restrictions are removed. Prices drop because a larger stockpile of units is available to meet demand. The marketplace looks at these regulations and figures out, even if the government hasn't, what the true impact on supply will be, and reacts accordingly.

11. DEMAND

The final leg of the CSD trio is demand–no more or less important a factor than condition or scarcity, but certainly the one most apt to change, and so the hardest to evaluate. Demand, even in a local area, can bounce around like a BB in a boxcar, being influenced by economic conditions, and time of the year and sometimes, I think, by the phase of the moon.

When we speak of "demand," we mean the buying public's interest in a particular make, model and variation of firearm, not one buyer's demand for a particular copy of that item. The first has to do with general interest; the second refers to a willingness to purchase one specific gun, in its existing condition, for a certain price.

The gun trader must also recognize two distinct sources of demand . . . one from the buying public, the "end user," and the other from competing gun traders. As unpredictable as the buying public can sometimes be, competing dealers can at times be absolutely confounding.

I recall attending a general auction some years ago at which two well-used .22 rifles were offered. The first was a semi-auto Savage Model 6, with its distinctive ventilated receiver, and the second was a single-shot bolt action. After a lengthy inspection, I realized that the bolt gun had been assembled from the components of at least two and possibly three rifles from different makers. The Savage, on the other hand, appeared to be in good operating condition. I've always liked this design, because it functions as both a single-shot and as an auto-loader. You push the operating handle in to lock the bolt closed for single work, or pull it out to allow it to blow back when functioning as a repeater.

I decided that I was not interested in the bolt gun, but would make an attempt to buy the Savage for, I believe, a maximum of $50. As I remember, the auction started at around $20, growing by $5 with each bid. By the time we got to my limit of $50, another bidder and I had exchanged several high bids, but I stopped at $50 and he took it at $55. Oh, well. I resumed watching the rest of the auction while he went to the side to collect his new Savage. Shortly thereafter, the auctioneer interrupted the flow of things to announce that the gun was going back up on the block . . . with the warning that it was assumed that bidders had carefully examined what they were bidding on!

So here we went again. He and I were the only bidders, and when he bailed out at $40, I bought the gun for $45. Still not quite understanding what had happened, I was sitting there with what was now my new Savage when the losing bidder came over and gloated, "Hey buddy, you paid too much for that, you know. It has a frozen breech and you'll have to pay to have it fixed."

His gloat disappeared when I pulled out the operating handle, cycled the bolt, and told him it seemed to be working okay. He was upset, to say the least. I could picture him tugging on the locked bolt during his inspection after the bidding, and his panicking when he concluded it was seized.

When the second gun came up, he'd apparently made up his mind that he wouldn't get outbid on this one. He and another bidder dueled it up to at least twice what it was worth, assuming that it even functioned. As he walked back to his seat with his prize, his face wore an expression of, "There, damn it."

When your competition abandons reason, it's time for you to walk away from the deal.

Demand is influenced by a whole array of things, and it is also unaffected by a lot of things. "Newest thing on the market" is probably at one end of the spectrum, with "stood the test of time" at the other end. In between is everything from politics to the environment to entertainment to, again, the phase of the moon.

There is a group of people who simply must own the newest, the biggest, the "baddest," or the fastest version of something on the market. Marketing people love this group, and were if not for these "early birds," the rest of the world might not see any changes at all. As gun traders, we need to be aware of this component of demand, even though we will not generally be dealing in the "newest" material.

Our need for awareness stems from the fact that, once a particular gun is no longer the "newest," the item is at a crossroads. It may go the way of the Dardick Tround and the Gyrojet, or it may catch on with the "followers." The point is that the gun really has no track record in the "used" market, and so we must evaluate demand based on gut feel, rather than on analysis.

The demand for firearms may also be affected by politics and events. In times of crisis, certain types of arms become more popular. That crisis could be anything from a September 11 scenario to a series of local burglaries. The potential election of a gun-friendly administration generally increases demand, as it is perceived that the ownership is politically correct. When an administration perceived to be anti-gun comes to town, there is often a flurry to purchase before new regulations take effect. If an outright ban with no grandfathering is anticipated, you may find people anxious to sell at reduced prices.

This desire to sell is of use to you, as a gun trader, only if you have a viable alternate market, as in another state or possibly even another country. I recall the story that made the rounds when the government of India announced a possession ban, to take effect in 30 days, on all rifles above a certain small caliber, for reasons of political security or some such nonsense. The ban included virtually every big-bore gun in the country, regardless of who owned it.

A quick-thinking Texan, who shall remain nameless, jumped on a plane with a bag of money and bought over 200 fine elephant and tiger rifles from the various maharajas, paying as little as $100 each. Many of these were ornate specimens, originally costing thousands of dollars. Did he take advantage of the situation? Absolutely! Did he take unfair advantage? Absolutely not! Any unfairness was on the part of the government. The maharajas, faced with a "low price or no price" choice, accepted the low price willingly. They had no time to find buyers outside of India, and there were none inside. Our Texan was creative, saw an opportunity, and seized it. He was able to do that because he was aware of the guns, aware of the new law, and aware of the demand for such guns in this country.

When southern New York State announced the opening of regular seasons on turkeys, demand skyrocketed for "turkey guns." Changing a locale from a rifle-hunting area to a shotguns-only area creates an instant market for "slug guns." Extending deer season by adding a muzzle-loading rifle period immediately ramps up the clamor for black-powder guns and coonskin caps. And closing seasons, or changing allowed weaponry, has the opposite effect. What do you suppose happens to the "deer rifles" in a newly announced "shotgun zone"? They become "trade bait," but because the retailer has no local market for them, their value drops. In steps the gun trader with alternate markets.

Even the competitive shooting sports themselves can affect demand. New competitions like sporting clays, three-gun team challenges (à la the old Chevy Truck events), and cowboy action shooting all modify demand for firearms. The sharp gun trader will understand how the demand picture has changed. For example, cowboy action shooting has pushed up prices on the all levels of original Western guns. Low- and medium-priced guns have been gobbled up in large numbers for the action shoots themselves. This in turn has put pressure on the remaining high-grade guns, as collectors are forced to chase fewer specimens. Additionally, the interest has spawned a whole series of reproduction guns that are less expensive than the originals, yet still maintain the heft and look.

Demand can also be funny in that sometimes folks just aren't interested. There is a group of older handguns known as "suicide specials," not to be confused with Saturday Night Specials. These "suicides" are small pocket revolvers, almost always in .22 rimfire, generally dating from the late 1800s to very early 1900s. They were usually well made, with spur triggers, small grips and, fairly often, nice engraving. Yet despite the fact that they show up in quite nice condition, there is relatively little interest in them from collectors, with the exception of a very few of the well-known names, like Smith and Colt. I've seen some fairly extensive collections of these little guns, all in nice condition, but they just don't spark any really enthusiastic collecting activity. For that reason, the prices are quite modest, all things considered.

So in light of all this, how do we evaluate demand? For starters, focus on the idea that we are not trying to determine what is "hot" in the market; we want to assess the current "hotness" of what we are looking at. It's perfectly OK to traffic in guns that are in only moderate demand, as long as we realize that fact, and as long as we buy and sell accordingly. Of particular importance is the understanding of the gun's near-term demand, because of our desire to turn the piece over quickly. It doesn't matter to you, the gun trader, what folks will want a year from now, but how much they will want this particular item in the next couple of months.

The problem with this is that your potential buyer is looking ahead and will be more motivated if he feels demand for his purchase will be growing in the future. Your job, tough as it may be, is to match up these seemingly opposed goals of buyer and seller. You'll often find that the key lies in the offering price, which we'll discuss in a later chapter.

Another pitfall to avoid, and we all give in to it to one extent or another, is projecting our own interests onto our customers. We love these old single shots, so others must also. How could you not want to have one of these gorgeous "black rifles"? And so on. It's perfectly okay to use that as part of the sales program, but it has no place in the assessment. Some folks feel that this ice-water approach takes the fun out of the game, but the successful gun trader will find a trade-off by having fun making bank deposits.

Watch out for the nostalgia trap, too You may have had a fantastic time hunting doves on the family farm with a light double just like this one, but don't let that blind you to either the condition of the gun you're holding or to the fact that your customer may not have similar experiences to draw on. The older you are, the younger you'll find your average customer to be. The more rural your upbringing, the more urban will be you average customer. Use all of those factors to create a framework for selling, but put them aside when you do your buying.

And speaking of age, let's be straight about something that will happen more and more as you move farther toward the crest of the hill. Gun prices have been moving steadily, and sometimes rapidly, upward for most of the last 50 years, but it is easy to forget that when we consider purchasing a model that's been around a long time. We remember the prices when the gun was introduced, and don't really accept the idea that a viable market for that gun can exist today at a much, much higher price, particularly since the model was discontinued for economic reasons.

One of my very first guns was a Savage Model 24 combination gun in 22LR/.410. I recall seeing ads back then listing the price as $49.95, and I still drag my feet when I see the gun today, even in excellent shape, with tags of $300 and up. Yet that original model is only infrequently encountered, and gets snapped up when it does show up. Perhaps it is the personal involvement that makes us hesitate, but I have often heard older gun traders remark, "that thing only cost $X when it came out . . . I know because I had one. How can somebody pay $6X for one?" Then they turn right around and ask top dollar on a gun from before their own time. This is one little quirk that everyone has to a degree, and we simply need to be aware of it.

SERIAL NUMBERS

Most firearms carry a serial number assigned by the manufacturer during production. There has been much made of the significance of serial numbers as they affect values, but in many cases, this impact is blown out of proportion. Generally, the serial number is of most use in establishing the date of manufacture. This can be important because it puts the firearm into a category such as "pre-War," "post-'64," "Civil War," "pre-acquisition," etc. Some of these categories are quite valid, and some have been invented by collectors.

When a serial number range represents a configuration, such as within a given model, the distinction can be important. For example, the Winchester Model 94 has been in continuous production since 1894, and while the designation has remained essentially the same, the firearm itself has had some important variations. In 1964, collectors perceived that the model had been "cheapened" by changing manufacturing techniques, part and material configurations, etc., and the "pre- and post-'64" Winchester categorization was born. Winchester realized the error of this model move, and has essentially revived the original Model 94 in terms of materials and manufacturing quality. They have retained some of the manufacturing technique changes which were made, and which have actually made the 94 a better arm. Nonetheless, these are still considered "post-'64" guns.

Another serial number range valuation occurs in the case of US Springfield 1903 rifles. Depending on the arsenal, rifles made before certain serial numbers were reached contained "brittle" receivers, which had a reputation for going to pieces. Low-number guns are often considered unfit for firing, while high numbers get a green light. There is undoubtedly some technical merit to this classification. You'll also see "pre-Garcia Sakos," "pre-warning Rugers," "Belgian" Brownings, and so on.

The point is that we need to recognize and understand, not necessarily agree with, these value categories when evaluating a potential purchase.

Some buyers place an emphasis on short serial numbers. The shortest serial number is, of course, #1, and that number will raise the value of virtually any gun associated with it. Of course, most #1s never got out of the plant. They often went to a company or government official, to the company museum, to the arm's designer, etc. Those coming onto the market have largely been snapped up by collectors. You are very unlikely to meet a real serial #1. So what about the next few numbers, such as 7, 16, etc?

I once owned Remington-Beals revolver #7, and believed that the Remington Arms Co. museum would be interested in it. They weren't. It seems they had a representative sample of the gun already, in nice shape, and it was the same gun as my #7, even though their serial number was higher. Makes sense. I also had a Colt Pocket percussion revolver carrying number 16. I didn't have it for long, because a collector wanted to own it quite a lot more than I wanted to keep it. He later told me that, at this point in the life of many Colt percussion pistols, the guns sometimes had odd barrel lengths, etc., as the production run was getting settled in. I never did have a chance to measure the barrel on that one, and he wouldn't ever tell me what he'd seen that got him so excited, but I did count the money several times. So should you encounter relatively low, or very low, serial numbers, know what the implication is. Know from your research whether there should be a premium added to the cost/price, and act accordingly. But never assume that there is such a premium just because the number is low.

HISTORIC FIREARMS

Let's face it, this is one area of firearms with which most of us are unlikely to become involved. It's true that virtually all guns have a history, but except for a minute fractional percentage of them, a) no one knows what that history is, and b) even if they did, no one would care.

Because we're trying to deal with primary sources when we can, our encounters with historical pieces will be determined in large part by where we live. Residents of Alaska and Hawaii are likely to find far fewer local specimens than are buyers from Massachusetts, South Carolina and Texas.

This may sound cold and cynical, but always start with the presumption that the piece is not of historical significance. No matter how much you would like to believe the nice little old lady, insist on documentation. Go after it yourself, if necessary, but until you have the provenance (documented origins) of the piece, presume that the specimen before you has been faked or doctored to increase its marketability. Prove to yourself that the gun is what it is, remembering that, as a defense attorney might say, "The absence of proof that something is fake is not proof that it is real."

The interest in historical pieces is natural, and the effect of provenance on the price of a gun can be quite remarkable. For example, an ordinary Walther pistol manufactured during WW II is of interest to military collectors. If that same pistol is found with markings indicating it was issued to a member of the Nazi party, the price jumps significantly. But were it discovered, with an inscription and ornamentation to the effect, that this gun was presented by the Walther firm to Hermann Goering, the price would simply go straight up.

The price has nothing whatever to do with the buyer's views on Nazi philosophy. It simply reflects a desire to own a piece of history. Wherever this sort of demand is present, someone is apt to give in to the temptation to meet it with fraudulent items, or a family member will add some luster to the resident folklore. So unless we simply decide that there is absolutely no way that we could ever be lucky enough to stumble across such a rarity (and none of us is apt to be of that mind, or we wouldn't be gun traders), we need to adopt the following approach: Attempt to prove conclusively that the gun is what the seller says it is. If we simply cannot do that, attempt to prove conclusively that the gun is not what the seller claims. Unless you can prove one or the other, it would be a mistake for you to pay anything extra for this "history," or to assume that your future buyer would, either.

Let's take the following as an example:

After Bat Masterson, the famous U.S. Marshal, left law enforcement and joined the staff of a widely read newspaper, he would keep an old Colt .45 in his desk. While talking with someone about the "old days," Bat would casually pull the gun out of the drawer and "allow as how he hardly carried this thing any more these days." The "pigeon" talking to him would start to drool and almost invariably begin negotiations for purchasing the gun. Bat, of course, would never "want to let it go," but eventually the buyer would wear him down and the gun would change hands . . . whereupon old Bat would go out and buy another one for his desk drawer.

There are probably more Colts documented as "once owned by Bat Masterson" than there are associated with any other Western figure. So let's pretend that you are offered such a gun, along with an old letter from Grandpa Johnson indicating that he had purchased Colt Peacemaker #12345 from Bat Masterson on June 5, 1912 for a price of $50.

Step One: Decide whether you are interested in purchasing a Colt owned by Bat Masterson, or looking for one carried by him when he was a Marshal. Why decide this? If you simply want a gun owned by Bat, you have one in front of you, if you believe what the letter says. Of course, this document will have virtually no effect on the value of the gun, unless you can prove that the letter is real. Therefore, you would offer to pay no more for this gun than you would for the same gun without the letter. But let's assume that you want to buy a gun carried by Bat while a marshal, and that the letter can be demonstrated to be the real thing. You know that he owned it, but how to determine when he owned it?

Step Two: Do some homework on Marshal Masterson. For starters, you'll learn that he lived from 1855 to 1921, so the letter could be real. But when and where was he active in law enforcement? Why? Because you are going to find out when the Colt was manufactured, and to what location it was first shipped. Clearly, if it was made after Bat left the job, he could not have carried it as a Marshal. He might well have owned it, but not as an officer of the law. (That's why Step One comes before Step Two.)

Step Three: Contact Colt or one of the historical collectors' groups for an official copy of the Colt factory records. Perhaps it will show shipment directly to Bat Masterson himself, but more likely it will reflect some wholesaler, if the data is available at all. The important thing is the date of manufacture, as this will not prove it was carried by Bat, but might show that it could not have been his. The location of the shipment may also be shown, and if it is to a Western city, that adds credibility to the provenance. If it went to Rhode Island or to Florida, chances are less that it found its way into the Marshal's possession.

Step Four: Carefully compare whatever information you can get from the factory records regarding the original configuration of the gun. If it left Connecticut with a 7 1/2″ barrel and now measures 4 3/4″, something has been changed. Probably not with any intent to defraud, but one never knows for sure. Any indication of ownership marked on the gun itself, as in the initials "B.M.," should cause an alarm to go off. Too much of a coincidence. (In the Walther example, a dedication to "Herman Goering" would also be a pretty good indication of fakery.)

Unfortunately, some of the rarer guns have been, and will continue to be, faked. Whenever you encounter a potentially rare or uncommon piece, discipline yourself to develop the proofs that the gun is or isn't what you would like it to be. ■

NOTES

BUY SMART
BUY LOW...

SUCCESSFUL BUYING

12. PRIMARY SOURCES

Now that we're all tooled up to go "gun hunting," where should we start to look? How about that gun show at the local armory tomorrow afternoon? Or what about a tour of the local gun shops? Maybe we hop onto Gunbroker.com or one of the other Internet auction sites? The newspaper classifieds?

If guns were going past us on some sort of conveyor belt, and all we had to do was pick out what we wanted, the answer would be far easier. Remember that our objective is maximum turn (consistent with our margin objectives), while at the same time keeping our stock of capital working. If you follow the techniques explained in the earlier chapters, you'll find that the biggest problem, surprisingly, is finding guns to buy rather than finding buyers for the guns on hand. In order to be sure that we don't pass up any opportunities, we'll be looking for guns everywhere, even where it's unlikely we'll find anything of interest. The trick is to use our time wisely, so let's establish a couple of guidelines to help us.

When a pre-owned gun comes onto the market, it moves up the "Price Pyramid" (see illustration on next page), with the old user at the bottom (Primary Source) and the new user at the top. In between are the resellers (Secondary Sources) who buy and sell guns for a profit. The more times a gun changes hands in moving from the old owner to the new owner, the more expensive it becomes, because each reseller adds his piece (reseller's premium) to the price.

A gun trader is one of those resellers. Ideally, we would like to be the only reseller between the old and new owners. Because there is only a certain amount of space in the pyramid from bottom to top, being the only reseller gives us maximum flexibility to make things work. Actually, each time a reseller is added, the pyramid becomes smaller, because the reseller takes on the role of the "old owner." We need to make a certain amount of profit on a given transaction, and as long as that profit can fit into the price pyramid between old and new owners, we have room to work.

As can be seen in the accompanying illustrations, we can buy at the bottom and sell below our target, or we can buy above bottom and sell at full target market, or we can work in between. Notice that we do not get piggy and try to buy at the bottom and sell at the top, because it makes our job tougher to do that way. We will develop this idea further in the pages ahead.

We want to spend the bulk of our time with sources at the bottom of the pyramid. These are the true primary sources. They will be either the owner/user, or variations on that theme . . . the inheritor, the widow/widower, the retiree, the relocator, the "cleaner-outer," the auctioneer, etc.

We want to focus on these sources as much as possible because they offer newly available material, and because we are not automatically paying that reseller's premium. Follow the local gun show circuit, wherever you live, and

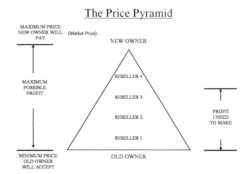

The Price Pyramid

you'll find certain dealers with the same basic stock at every show. Some pieces you'll see at show after show . . . no new material. Select one of these "well traveled" pieces and make an offer below the asking price. Likely as not, you'll hear "can't do that, I've got to make something on it." That "something" he's talking about is the reseller's premium, but more importantly, this is an example of not having the flexibility, or the sense, to make a deal and cut his losses. Positioning ourselves correctly in the Price Pyramid gives us the flexibility to make a deal if we have to, but using the TEK system greatly reduces the number of situations where such dealing becomes necessary.

One of my favorite true stories about primary sources involves a fellow (call him Jack) who did "light hauling" on evenings and weekends. Basically, if you wanted the garage or attic or basement cleaned out (emptied), Jack would charge a small fee, back up the pickup and haul away. His thinking was that "lots of good stuff gets thrown away." And he was right. He would keep the good stuff and dump the rest. One day, Jack received a call from a lady in an exclusive little enclave in southern New York State. She was the recent widow of a very well-off business tycoon and was selling the estate. Would he come over and haul out the junk in the basement? Yes, indeed!

He took away quite a few loads of "old good stuff," but commented to me a few weeks later that the basement had contained a surprise. Along one wall, in about a dozen shiny galvanized containers, were about 150 to 200 long guns. Jack was a collector of many things, including guns, and it really bothered him to see those pieces displayed that way, but, as he put it, "when you've got the bucks, you can be as eccentric as you want to be, and treat things any way you want." I asked him how many he'd bought, and he answered "I can't even guess at how much she would have wanted, but I bet I couldn't have afforded even a few of them. I didn't even talk to her about buying them."

Some months afterward, another lady in the same area called looking for a haul-out, and Jack gave her the first lady's name (Mary) as a reference. When he hadn't heard back from the second lady, he called her to see when she wanted him to get started, and was told that the reference has proven so negative that she'd hired someone else. "All Mary did was tell me again and again how upset she was that you never finished the job."

Needless to say, Jack was floored. By then, Mary had sold the place and relocated, but he finally pieced together what had gone wrong. The shiny galvanized containers in the basement were newly purchased garbage cans and she had literally stuffed them with her late husband's collection. She wanted nothing to do with them, and had called Jack to get rid of them, along with the rest of the "good stuff." Unfortunately, Mary didn't mention the guns specifically, only telling Jack to "clean out the basement." She was upset because she'd had to call another hauler in just to take out the guns. Jack told me later that the idea of the guns being available, much less free for the taking, was so far into the realm of the unlikely that it hadn't even occurred to him to make an inquiry.

So let's keep Mary and Jack in mind as we look at primary sources.

The Basic Owner-User: This one is real simple . . . for sale by owner. Maybe he just wants to sell, maybe he has to sell, and maybe he needs cash to trade up to another gun. Whatever the reason, he is motivated to find a buyer. You are motivated to find a seller. The owner-user will naturally want to get the most for what he has, so you may not always be able to strike a deal. He recalls what he paid at retail for the gun, or has seen the current value listed in a reference book. You know what the market for resale is. Work together and see what you come up with.

Other primary sources will include:

The Inheritor: This person (could be a son/daughter, grandson/daughter, cousin, etc.) can be a most interesting primary source because he/she often has no attachment to the pieces offered, and consequently will let them go near the bottom end of the "offer range." If the number of guns available is large, as in the situation of liquidating a collection, the buying can sometimes be extended over a period of time. Usually, though, you'll want to make the deal before the seller changes his mind or gets a higher offer from someone else.

The Widow/er: Let me start here be saying that I consider it unethical to pursue the newly bereaved in order to make a purchase. Beyond that, however, when she has come to you, the situation will be much as with the inheritor, except that the widow may be fearful (and rightly so) of being "taken." She wants to get the best price she can, but doesn't have any real idea of worth, and so may be unsure or confused. This is where your references and reputation come into play.

The Retiree/Relocator: These folks are making life changes, and sometimes will have guns that just don't fit in. A snowbird heading for Florida from northern Minnesota will probably not have much use for his old deer gun, but don't expect him to dump his small-gauge double. Up until the early'90s, most retiring big-city police officers had two revolvers to sell, a Smith & Wesson Model 10 and a Smith Model 36 (or the Colt equivalents). Occasionally there is also a time incentive for the person to sell . . . as in "we're moving next week." Our evaluation system will allow you to make swift decisions in this type of situation.

The "Cleaner-Outer": If you can find one of these folks (remember Jack and Mary?), he/she could be a real gold mine, particularly if you stick with our system and resist the urge to low-ball him. It isn't as important that you buy everything from him, as long as you are the first to see everything he gets his hands on. Unless he is actually a collector himself, he might be very happy to have a fair, ready market for any guns that come his way . . . the old "fast nickels before slow dimes" idea.

The Auctioneer: It's true that auctioneers are in the game to make money, and so might not be considered primary sources, but remember that auctioneers come in two flavors: those from whom you buy, and those who come to you for your expertise. Get to know your local auction houses, especially those that handle firearms. Get to know the auctioneers themselves. Remember that you are a specialist, while they must be generalists. The guns you are looking for will not usually be run-of-the-mill pieces, and since you will be an expert in your specialty area, you can be of immense value to the auctioneer as a source of information on what the item is and what it should sell for. Once again, the idea is not necessarily to buy everything, or anything, from him. The idea is to be aware of everything he has available. And estate auctioneers will often suggest "private placements" to their clients. Be ready should that opportunity arise.

It won't happen too often, but once in a while you'll hit an auction where a few guns are on the block and the crowd is just not interested. If there's no reserve on the bidding (a reserve is just a sneaky way of getting a minimum price), you might just find yourself in heaven. I recall one auction, on a cold, rainy autumn night, which listed about a dozen guns, including a Ruger .308 bolt rifle. I went to the auction just to see what the traffic would bear, and with no real expectations of buying anything. Along with the Ruger and several .22s and standard shotguns was a Remington 1889 12 ga. double in beautiful condition under a light coat of grime. I mentally appraised the gun to sell for $300-$350 and settled back to watch the action.

The auctioneer opened the bidding for "this old rabbit-eared shotgun" (first clue that this could be a good night) for $50 (second clue). Even after the bidding opened at $25, no one was interested in the gun. Finally, I bought the gun for $65, and sold it three days later for $375!

Great story, but what had actually happened? All of the gun buyers in the house were focusing on the Ruger .308. Bidders were waving like they were dockside for the Queen Mary. The combination of bad weather and an audience of end-users (they were bidding on a rifle for their own use) created a great opportunity for me. By the way, the Ruger sold for just over retail.

If you do decide to try your hand at an auction, get there early, inspect every-thing under good light, stay within your area of expertise and do your "figuring out" first. Be sure you know what the total price will be, including the "buyer's premium" if there is one. The "BP" is tacked onto the final bid, and at the usual 10 percent-15 percent, can add up on the more expensive pieces. It's the creative auctioneer's way of taking a smaller cut from the selling party without taking a smaller cut for the auc-tioneer. Never, ever, bid on a gun you haven't examined closely, now matter how the auctioneer describes it. Pay attention to the bidding, but don't get caught up in the excitement. When the bidding passes your pre-determined level, pull your hand down! And finally, once the bidding starts, never wave to a friend across the room. Otherwise, you can wind up owning some really strange and expensive stuff.

By the same token, once you've made up your mind to bid, don't jump out before you hit your max price. I came home one afternoon and my wife told me that "Bob" had called that morning. When I returned his call, he said, "I was calling you from an auction this morning to see what a gun was worth. It was a Parker double, 20 gauge, fitted case, and two sets of barrels. I'm not sure of the grade, but I know it wasn't marked Trojan and it didn't have Damascus barrels. I was afraid of bid-ding too much on it."

I told him that it sounded like a great gun and he probably didn't need to worry about overpaying.

"Well, I'm afraid that I might have made a mistake," he replied.

"Seriously, Bob, you won't have any trouble at least getting your money out. They're in heavy demand, especially in the condition you described."

"No, I really think I made a mistake on it."

When I told him, "Bob, the only mistake you could have made would have been to let it get away from you," there was a long pause. "You DID buy it, didn't you, Bob?"

Finally he replied, "No, I stopped bidding before it sold." He sounded so low that I tried to cheer him up with, "Well, you know, sometimes the other guy wants it so badly that he's just willing to go higher than you can afford." (I knew that Bob was doing very well financially, so this was about the only comforting thought I could come up with.) "What did it finally go for?"

After an even longer pause than before, he said quietly, "$200."

Now, Bob had been a shooter and hunter for many years. He knew the Parker name, he knew that quality doubles were in demand, and he had plenty of money to work with. He just plain chickened out. Still in shock, I closed our conversation with "Well, don't be too hard on yourself. All that happened was that you blew the opportunity of a lifetime."

The Counselors: This group would include attorneys, insurance agents, morticians, physicians and clergy. I've included them under Primary Sources because they are usually directly associated with "original owners." You would be surprised how often they are asked for referrals on disposing of firearms.

Attorneys have to deal with divorces, court orders, etc. Insurance agents sometimes find that their clients don't want to pay extra for a rider to cover their guns, but don't want to keep them without coverage, either. Morticians, physicians and clergy are frequently called upon to give advice on disposing of arms once the owner has passed away. Out of the whole "counselor" group, most of your referrals will probably come from clergy, perhaps because, rightly or wrongly, clergy are often more trusted than lawyers and insurance agents. The leader of one congregation talks to the leader of another (usually within the same denomination, but sometimes they "cross party lines") and your reputation as an honest and knowledgeable buyer gets around quickly. Trust me on this one . . . spend some effort in developing these "counselor" contacts.

13. SECONDARY SOURCES

Secondary sources include wholesalers, dealers/retailers, pawnbrokers and auction houses, and the most important thing to remember about secondary sources is that they will always increase your costs. That's how they make their money. They got to the original owner before you did, and now they're getting paid for that extra effort.

That said, however, we may still find ourselves doing business with a secondary source. Remember the idea of standing beside a conveyor belt of guns, picking and choosing what we wanted as the belt moved past? Well, sometimes wholesalers and retailers, especially retailers, help bring us closer to that reality, especially in the form of large used-gun departments and gun shows. We may not find the asking prices as we would like them, but at least we can see what is available. Then we need decide whether it falls into our expertise niche (what's the market), our discount niche (where should I price it for my profile?) and our stake niche (can I afford it?). Sometimes you can reach an accommodation with a retailer, once he realizes that you are a volume buyer with funds. Given your license status, he may also see you as a sale with less paperwork, and therefore requiring less of his time.

We've already talked about auctioneers under Primary Sources. Again, know what your bid means in terms of a final price, be bold, but don't get caught up in the action. One service that auctioneers can provide is their auction catalog, especially when it includes a follow-up "prices realized" list. This allows you to see how things played out at that time, in that place.

A similar type of bid tracking can be had by flagging items on the Internet auction sites. This is especially desirable in the case of high-end guns, the market for which can be quite volatile.

A pawnbroker can sometimes be a good secondary source, as long as you are dealing with a reputable one. If you've not dealt with a "hock shop" before, the transaction goes something like this:

You bring your item to the broker, who agrees to lend you money, holding the item as security. He gives you a receipt (pawn ticket) that says you have the right to redeem the item within, say, 30 days, for the loan amount plus a markup. He agrees to hold the item for that number of days, waiting for you to redeem it. After the time has expired, he is free to sell the item at whatever price he can get. For you as a gun trader, he becomes a secondary source once the redemption time has expired.

Remember, the pawnbroker makes his money by turning it over, just like you do. Toward that end, he may pay only a minimal price to the "pawner." He can still make his money and sell at an attractive price. He knows that when his money is tied up in guns, it can take longer to turn because of licensing, etc. That's good for you, because your license will make you a more attractive customer.

To turn it more quickly though, he may also be tempted to cut some corners . . . like paperwork. That's bad for you. At least stop by the shops in your area. You'll quickly get a good idea of what sort of person the broker is. In order to deal in firearms, pawnbrokers must hold a Federal Firearms License (FFL), plus whatever additional permits are required by state and local agencies. An up-and-up broker will not knowingly take in "hot" merchandise, but should something later turn out to be amiss, the authorities are going to want to reverse the transaction chain, returning the gun to its rightful owner. You don't get into legal trouble, but at a minimum you lose the profit you made on your later sale.

Additionally, guns found at pawnshops will often be sort of on the down-and-out side This is another way of saying that if you find a pristine high-end piece under "the sign of the three globes," tread very carefully. Ask the questions and listen to the answers. A reputable pawnbroker will understand your hesitation and will not be offended by the questions. If you sense any hedging, run, don't walk, for the exit. But if everything seems okay, and the potential purchase fits your profile, go for it.

14. ADDING VALUE: CLEANING

As you travel about the countryside looking for potential gun purchases, you will encounter guns which "will clean up nicely," or that need a little adjustment or a small part. This will likely happen sooner rather than later. An awful lot of the guns trading hands out there, especially those from primary sources, could use some kind of "TLC." Without question, if you were buying for your own use, you'd provide that care, and we know that if we have two copies of the same gun side by side, the one in better condition will command the higher price. So why, after making a purchase for resale, wouldn't you try to think of ways to add to its value? Because as a gun trader, your motto is "buy right to sell right," so you are going to do all of that thinking before you make the purchase, not after.

Adding value simply means that we are going to make an investment of effort and/or money in the gun that, we hope, will increase its market value. We're going to add to our cost, in hopes of adding more than that cost to the selling price. Here are some basic guidelines for deciding whether "to clean or not to clean."

GUIDELINES FOR ADDING VALUE

You are a gun trader, first and foremost, not a gunsmith. Even if you enjoy the tinkering end of the game, you should consider the "adding value" question from a gun trader's perspective.

1. Repair, modification, adjustment—literally anything beyond wiping a gun down with a silicone cloth—costs you time (and therefore money), and perhaps also out-of-pocket money. All of these costs have to be considered in figuring the purchase/selling price of the gun.

2. If you do cleanings or repairs yourself, you will reduce the time you have for buying and selling. If you pay someone else to do the work, you increase the total cost of the gun.

3. It takes time to perform repairs, whether done by you or by another party. While the gun is "in the shop," it is not available for sale, and so cannot be "turned."

4. If you make repairs that were not considered in the purchase decision, you will add cost to the deal, which may or may not be recoverable through a higher selling price, but in either case, it is unlikely that you will meet your timetable for sale.

TWO EXAMPLES

A primary source finds, in a corner of the barn, a Parker shotgun in 12 gauge. The wood is sound, but because the gun has been standing muzzle down, there is considerable rusting and pitting inside and out on the barrels. The gun is a potential candidate for a complete restoration, including replacement of the barrel tubes. You project a total cost of several thousand dollars and six months for a qualified restorer to do the job. Do you have it restored, do you sell to a buyer "as is," or do you pass on the deal?

At a yard sale, you find a Remington bolt-action single-shot .22, vintage 1955. The metal is smooth, the finish about 90 percent blue. The wood has a good figure, and the varnish is original and also about 90 percent complete. The bolt is missing, however. You find a complete replacement bolt on eBay for $75.00. Do you buy the gun, and if so, how much do you offer?

These examples are presented only to demonstrate the kind of decisions you'll be making.

HOW TO CLEAN AND HOW MUCH

Cleanup is probably the most frequently used means of adding value to a firearm. A clean arm will command a higher price than will a dirty one, and it will also sell faster. So the idea is to take anything we purchase, hit it with solvent and steel wool, maybe even a bit of sandpaper for the rust spots, and get it looking like a million dollars. The brighter the gun, the higher the price. Right? Of course, not.

Any firearm, regardless of age, should look well cared for. New-in-the-box arms should be factory-perfect in every regard. A 100-year-old shotgun will have a different look.

Examine a fine old double that has been a family's prized possession for several generations. You'll see that it is mechanically tight and sound, with absolutely no sign of abuse or neglect. The bores will be spotless, the metal free of any rust or pitting. The gun will be clean, inside and out. The wood will show careful maintenance, with no softening from over-oiling. This is not to say that all of the finish will be perfect. Some of the blue may be worn from handling, or there may be an old touch-up of a briar scratch on the wood. The checkering at the wrist may be worn, but it will be sound. In a nutshell, the gun does not look new, it looks well-cared for. Keep this idea in mind as we continue.

A sculptor was once asked how he had been able to create, from a huge block of marble, such a magnificent statue of a famous cavalryman on his rearing charger. His reply was—and this is our guideline in firearms cleaning—"I just started at the top and cut away the parts that didn't look like General Custer and his horse." He took away what wasn't supposed to be there, and left behind what was. As we clean a firearm, that will be our approach also.

Most of the guns we encounter will have metal finished with some sort of oxide finish. Oxide is the result of a chemical process called oxidation, which is a fancy name for rust. It occurs when the metal comes in contact with one of a variety of chemicals or compounds in the presence of oxygen, and the observable result is a change in color.

The color varies with the metal and the chemical . . . black, red, brown, blue, green, gray, etc. These finishes are attractive, but they have a more important function. Once the oxide layer has formed, it protects the base metal from further chemical action. Think of it as rusting that has been allowed to begin, then stopped before any pitting occurs. (Example: Leave a brightly polished garden trowel out in the rain for a couple of days, then bring it in and wipe it off. You'll see that the metal is still smooth, but has a dark reddish staining. Presto . . . an oxide finish.) Once that finish is allowed to reach a certain depth, say .002 inches, further exposure will not create new rust.

So why do we care about all this? When we clean up a gun with an oxide finish, we will want to remove the junk, crud, dirt, call it what you will, that is sitting on top of the oxide layer. We want to take off the dirt, but not the blue. Here's the problem: On many older guns, and so on many of the more expensive pieces we'll encounter, there is a very thin layer between the dirt and the oxide. This is called patina. Patina is basically a change in the color of the oxide coating caused by age

These replaceable tip pin punches can get into tight places for disassembly, and are also available in a shorter "starter" version. Be sure to pick up some spare pins in case of breakage. CREDIT: BROWNELLS

A bench block like the one shown provides solid support for your gun, yet allows you to insert or remove a pin easily. The nylon body is non-marring and seems to last forever. CREDIT: BROWNELLS

(and only age!). When this same situation appears on a modern gun, it is properly called rust staining, and is not acceptable. Gun traders have learned to expect patina on an elderly piece and, in fact, will usually downgrade the price when patina has been removed.

The problem presents itself from a different angle in the case of a gun finished "in the bright," as many military arms were in the 1800s. There is no original oxide coating, but the exposure to air over so many decades still results in a patina (actually a faint oxide coating in itself). So our task is to remove the dirt without disturbing the patina. Easily said, but very tough to do. And for this reason, many gun traders elect to discount both purchase offer and sales price, leaving the delicate cleanup for the buyer to deal with.

Whether or not to disassemble the gun is our first decision. Again, you're a gun trader, not a 'smith, so the idea is to be as efficient with your time as possible. Remember that disassembly always carries with it the danger of breakage or inadvertent scratching.

If you must break the gun down, do so into large chunks, rather than pulling out every pin and screw. Have on hand the proper basic tools of the trade, including a bench block, vise pads, pin punches and hammers with forgiving faces. Use a good set of parallel ground screwdriver bits, such as those from Brownells, and select the bit that fits the screw slot in both length and width. Steel on steel can leave marks, no matter how careful you are. Where possible, use brass, plastic, nylon or wood on steel.

Bits are retained in the Magna-Tip screwdriver by a strong magnet. The bits are hollow ground, in a variety of lengths and widths. They come in thick, thin, and extra extra-thin versions and offer a choice of regular, torx, phillips, and allen points. Your basic Magna-Tip set can be augmented with many different additional tips. CREDIT: BROWNELLS

Using these roll-pin punches great-ly lessens the chance of damaging your roll pins during assembly and disassembly. The special tip keeps the punch from sliding off the pin and scratching the gun during re-assembly.

Replacement screw sets can be useful in repairing damage caused by poorly fitted screwdrivers. For a proper appearance, artificial "aging" may be necessary. Generally, it's better to retain original screws when you can.CREDIT: BROWNELLS

Use a toothpick or toothbrush to clean out the screw slot before you try to move the screw the first time. Many beginners, and some folks who should know better, skip that step and wind up with a scratched receiver, or a burred or broken screwhead. If you must pull the screw, let the metal-to-metal joint soak in a little Breakfree solvent first, unless the screw turns with only gentle pressure. Remember, though, that even the milder solvents can damage the patina layer.

And no matter how careful you are, if you remove enough screws, sooner or later a screwhead is going to break off. It simply is going to happen, given enough time, putting you up the proverbial creek. For this reason, if no other, avoid disassembly when you can.

Cleanup materials will include a soft cloth, a mild solvent such as original Hoppe's #9, one of the ammoniated heavy-duty bore cleaners like Sweet's, tooth-picks, regular gun oil, some Breakfree, and maybe a wad of #0000 steel wool. If you have access to an ultrasonic cleaner, that's a good way to handle the internals should they need de-gumming, and it may save you from having to do a full disas-sembly. Use the steel wool as a last resort, and always use it lightly. Its job is to assist the oil or solvent. The #0000 grade will not harm the bluing, but it can thin

In addition to the usual ball peen bench ham-mer, the gun trader will also find plenty of uses for specialized ham-mers, such as the rawhide or nylon/brass styles shown. CREDIT: BROWNELLS

or reduce the patina layer, so be extremely careful. When in any doubt with cleaning, less is better. This paragraph applies to the external metal and to the internal moving parts. The bore is a different matter.

All bores left the factory or armory sparkling bright. Properly maintained, they will be that way 100 years later, so a dark bore is never a good thing. Under the NRA grading system, a bore's condition is disregarded for antiques, but a bright bore will always outsell a dark one, everything else being equal. You can't overdo a bore cleaning, as long as you don't scratch it, and as long as you don't damage the muzzle area. Even a pitted shotgun bore looks better when it's bright. The buyer will know someone polished it up (or it wouldn't have pitted to begin with), but it will still be a better seller.

Hoppe's #9 will clean a bore, given enough effort, but there also exist today a group of industrial-strength kicked-up ammonia-boosted bore cleaners, including Sweets, Shooter's Choice, Accu-bore, and others. These super brews can be powerful stuff, so be careful to keep them in the bore, because they can lift patina in a heartbeat. They're designed to quickly cut through fouling of all types, but can sometimes play havoc with wood finishes and even some of the more delicate metal finishes. Minimize the spatter, mop up spills quickly, and absolutely keep them off the stock.

There are also several electrolytic de-plating systems on the market that essentially pull the fouling off the bore and redeposit it on the bore rod. The main bugaboo with these cleaners involves getting a good current flow within the electrolyte. You have to spend time fiddling to get the electrical contact solid without scratching the metal with the contact clamp. Also, electronic bore cleaners are expensive for only occasional use, but properly hooked up, they do work.

Regardless of whether you use elbow grease or electricity, get the bore as clean as you can . . . and factor that cleaning into your calculation of the gun's cost.

Our work at cleaning up the stock will be much more limited, particularly on the older guns. If the wood needs restoration, factor the time and cost into the purchase decision, have it done professionally and move along to the next purchase. Otherwise, limit the work to a wipe-down with a clean soft cloth. No solvent, no oil, and by all means, no solvent or stock finish of any kind. Why? Because wood patina is even more delicate than metal patina. It can be damaged very quickly, and that damage will be very obvious. Be careful around the checkering to avoid snagging a splinter with a cloth fiber, and be sure to clean any residual lint from the wood-metal creases.

15. ADDING VALUE: REPAIRS
(WHEN AND WHEN NOT TO MAKE THEM)

If you have already decided not to consider purchasing firearms that need repair in one form or another, feel free to skip right over this section. But also be prepared to work harder to get enough guns into your pipeline. Out of three pre-owned guns that you find available from primary sources, two will probably benefit from cleaning or repair of some type. Since we are professional and expert gun traders, not professional and expert gunsmiths, we need to decide which ones we do ourselves, which we have done by someone else, and which we walk away from.

The costs of the repair include:

a) The cost of any purchased parts or services;

b) Any time you spend looking for or ordering those services;

c) All time and money spent in moving the gun to/from a common carrier;

d) All shipping charges;

e) The cost of having money tied up in the gun while it is being repaired.

All these costs become a part of the purchase price, with an appropriate mark-up added.

All time spent ordering parts, etc., should have a cost assigned so it can be added to the purchase price. Unless you already know how long a repair will take, assume at least one hour for even the smallest of repair efforts, including set-up, actual work time and cleanup. In order to properly cost your time, sell it to yourself at the same rate as you would pay to someone else. If the local 'smith would charge $40 to replace that worn pad, assign the same cost to the time it takes to do it yourself (assuming you can do the job as well and as quickly).

Use the same approach for cleaning, chamber casting, installing new grips on a pistol, adding a plug screw, etc. If you aren't sure what rate to use, look at the Brownells catalog for their periodic industry-wide survey of shop prices. Each type of work is listed with a range of prices charged. Pick one in the middle for your use. In fact, it's a good idea to add $10 or $20 to any purchase price just to cover the wipe-downs, etc. that will be required, even if no "repairs" as such are needed.

RECOIL PADS

If you are buying long guns, particularly shotguns, that are more than about 30 years old, you'll probably find that many of the recoil pads are disintegrating or are at least hardened to the point of being both non-functioning and unsightly. This is mostly due to age, along with exposure to solvents that didn't exist when these pads were first developed.

These ugly pads really detract from the salability of any gun, and most are candidates for replacement. This is not a complex job, but it does require care and a little patience. You can set up to do the work yourself, or you can pay a smith to it. Many gunsmiths don't really like to do replacement pads unless they are also refinishing or replacing the stock, so this is one repair that may make sense to try on your own.

The installation technique is basically the same no matter which pad you use. The time-eater is the filling of old screw holes and drilling of new ones. Sometimes you get lucky with the hole match-ups, and sometimes you don't, but don't cut any corners here because it will absolutely show up in the finished product. With the exception of the hole alignment, if the old pad was factory installed, it is likely that with the old pad removed, the buttstock is ready to accept a new one.

But if the old job was a less-than-professional installation, you may have to do some work with a sanding disc or block to square and flatten the end of the butt-stock. If you do any sanding, be sure to reseal the end grain of the wood with Tru-Oil or a similar sealer.

Take care in selecting the replacement pad. Try to come as close to the original in color and style as you can. Before starting the replacement work, study the recoil pad installation directions found in "Gun Kinks" from Brownells in Montezuma, Iowa. Most pad makers, such as Pachmayr, offer several sizes in each model. Purchase based on their sizing recommendation, not on how much pad has to be trimmed away. Invariably, when trimming work is minimized, the pad has insufficient length to carry the lines of the stock through to the toe of the pad. Rather than working freehand, use a fitting jig. In addition to keeping the edges square, these jigs do the work away from the stock, so there is no chance of scratching the original finish.

Some of the manufacturers are offering remakes of the originals pads, especially the Winchester solid-rubber pad, and these reproductions should be considered whenever you can find them. Just remember that every pad has to be fitted . . . regardless of what the packaging says. Also, never try to pass off a new pad as an original. Sooner or later, the customer will find out, and your reputation depends on customer trust.

BUTTPLATES AND GRIP CAPS

Many of the hard buttplates and/or grip caps you'll run into will be quite ornate, made of hard rubber . . . and cracked or broken. Sometimes you can find a repro of the original plate, such as the dog's head plate on Parkers. Many other times, you're faced with a repair. This isn't so bad if you have all of the pieces, but when a chunk is missing, you'll need to fill in the spot or replace the whole plate. The fitting technique is similar to that used for butt pads, and most of the same equipment can be used. Curved plates are more complicated.

Think about that when considering a relatively inexpensive gun with this type of damage (like a Stevens Favorite). Even if you have access to a box full of old buttplates, you may find some that are close, but you will not find one that fits, and fitting will still be needed. So don't buy a gun with the idea of just finding a replacement that will fit properly. It won't happen.

Plug screws are available in either the dome-style, as shown, or in the traditional flat flat-top version. If you mount a scope on a gun, be sure to save the factory plug screws for possible later use later on.

CREDIT: BROWNELLS

PLUG SCREWS

A plug screw is simply a headless screw used to fill an unused hole drilled in a barrel or receiver. These are often installed at the factory when sights or scope mounts are not furnished. Most American screws of this nature are standard sizes, but when you hit European pieces, anything goes. Some manufacturers, such as Remington, use a plug screw that actually has a slightly domed head. Try to use originals in this type of replacement.

In installing or removing any plug screw, make sure that the bit is thin enough to get down in the slot, and narrow enough to not touch the outside of the screw hole. Clean them with solvent, and if you know the thread size, consider cleaning out the hole with the correct tap. This does take a little time, but probably not enough to make it worth giving the work to your smith.

DAMAGED SCREW HEADS

Which is better . . . a damaged screw head that screams "abuse," or a shiny new screw head that, on an older gun, screams "replacement"? When you can, change the damaged screws. Several companies are offering complete replacement screw sets for specific guns. If necessary, learn to "age" a screw head to match the surrounding metal (and let the customer know that it is a replacement). Realize that the head is damaged for a reason, and could be "frozen" in place.

SCREW CHECKER

BROWNELLS

Orders: 800-741-0015 Office: 641-623-5401
Fax: 641 623 3896 www.brownells.com
300 SOUTH FRONT STREET
MONTEZUMA, IA 50171

SIZE	N.C. TAP	N.F. TAP	N.S. TAP	DIA
1 (DRILLS → 48)	64 (53)	72 (53)		.073
2 (DRILLS → 43)	56 (51)	64 (50)	SCREW	.086
3 3/32 (38)	48 (47)	56 (45)	CHEK'R	.099
4 (DRILLS → 33)	40 (43)	48 (42)	36 (43)	.112
5 1/8 (30)	40 (39)	44 (37)	U.S. PAT. 2728145	.125
6 5/32 (28)	32 (36)	40 (33)	48 (35)	.138
8 23 (DRILLS → 19)	32 (29)	36 (29)	40 (28)	.164
10 3/16 (DRILLS → 10)	24 (25)	32 (21)		.190
12 7/32 (DRILLS → 7/32)	24 (16)	28 (14)	32 (13)	.216
1/4	20 (8)	28 (3)	32 (7/32)	.250
9/32 1/4	18	24	32	.312
5/16 (DRILLS → 5/16)	(F)	(I)	(9/32)	

WHITWORTH 55° *WEST-GERMANY*

Gun screws come in a variety of diameters and threadings, so this screwchecker helps you make sure you are using the correct replacement size. It can also be used to clean up tiny burrs at the end of a shortened screw. Also shown is a thread gauge, necessary for identifying threads not covered by the screwchecker. A thread gauge is especially useful when working with older guns or those with metric screws. CREDIT: BROWNELLS

BEADS AND SIGHTS

These are not necessarily difficult repairs, but there is some specialized equipment needed to do the job quickly and cleanly, and so you may not want to get that involved. Removing the old part is sometimes the toughest part of the job. Be sure your smith knows what he, or she, is doing, as experience means a lot to the finished appearance. Be sure that the bead used is correct for the gun, both in height and style. Understand that new plastic will not look as good as old ivory, no matter how hard you work at it, but it may be the best solution available.

These aluminum and brass beads are easy to install and make excellent repairs for damaged sights on your shotgun. Use the white plastic version for replacing ivory beads. CREDIT: BROWNELLS

A bead installer is faster and easier to use than fingers or pliers, and eliminates the danger of scratching the barrel or marring the bead. These are available in several sizes to fit a variety of bead diameters. CREDIT: BROWNELLS

Scratches to the gun and damage to the sight are much less likely when using a sight pusher, rather than driving the sight in or out with a hammer and punch. Some pushers are fitted with bushings for specific sights and can move either left or right. Others, like the Williams model, (on the right) are "push-only" and work in a wide variety of situations. CREDIT: BROWNELLS

Rifle sights for inexpensive .22s offer more latitude, but you'll need originals or copies of them for the higher-grade guns. Often, manufacturers used sights made by one of the major sight companies, and they're what should be used to replace the damaged or missing parts. Be sure you use the correct height for both front and rear sights, as this is critical to having sufficient adjustment range. Guiding principle here: If you're going to do it, do it right. Otherwise, leave the part as it is and discount the deal accordingly.

CHAMBER CASTS

The reason you are doing a chamber cast is that you are unsure of either the chamber length or the cartridge. The materials are not expensive and the technique is simple, so learn to do this one yourself. You should already have a good caliper, preferably digital, but if you don't, get one to do this work.

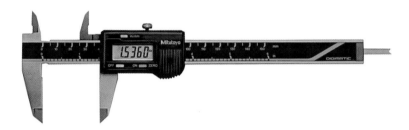

The serious gun trader needs a good caliper, either dial or digital. Buy the very best you can afford and take good care of it. The digital type is the easier to use, but dial calipers are gentler on your wallet. CREDIT: BROWNELLS

SHOTGUN CHAMBER LENGTHENING

Within certain strict limits, there is an opportunity to add some significant value to certain older shotguns by lengthening the chambers slightly to accommodate modern shell lengths. The reason for considering doing this job is that it may make a shooter out of a wall hanger. There are plenty of ways to get into trouble here, so if you are going to do the work yourself, be absolutely certain that you understand how to evaluate chamber and forcing cone wall thickness, how to properly use a chamber reamer, etc. Be guided by the instructions provided by tech experts, such as those at Brownells.

Since you will be changing the original specification of the gun, you'll take a price hit on originality, but get a return for increasing the utility of the gun. Even with that return, you wouldn't do this work on a gun in top condition. Lengthening the average chamber and forcing cone will take perhaps an hour or so, and this has to be figured into the cost/price equation. Refer to the Appendix for specific directions on chamber lengthening.

These shotgun chamber reamers from Brownells lengthen the chamber and cut a longer forcing cone at the same time. Be absolutely sure that you have enough wall thickness remaining after the reaming. CREDIT: BROWNELLS

Barrel liners, or inserts, like these can bring new shooting life to old .22's and other guns. Relining reduces the "originality" of the gun, but may enhance the market value, depending on exterior condition. CREDIT: BROWNELLS

RELINING BARRELS ON .22 RIFLES AND HANDGUNS

You are going to encounter a recurring problem with .22 rifles from the black-powder cartridge era: The barrels will usually be in poor shape, primarily from the corrosive effects of the powder/priming used back then. Bores on Stevens Favorites, Scouts, Crackshots, along with their littermates and competitive rivals, are very often candidates for being drilled out and relined. The job is not complicated, but it takes time, effort and some special tools. The good part is that, again, it can make a shooter out of something that might otherwise be reduced to parts.

As with chamber lengthening in shotguns, limit relining to those specimens in less than good condition. The basic ideal of relining is that you will drill out the existing bore to accept a thin pre-rifled liner tube. This will be held in place with epoxy or solder. The liner will then be trimmed to length and the extractor slots and chamber re-cut. For more detailed and specific direction on barrel relining, contact Brownells, 200 Front Street, Montezuma, IA, Brownells and ask them for a copy of *.22 Caliber Barrel Lining Instructions & Equipment.*

As an alternative to the chamber and barrel work listed here, if you find that your sources are supplying you with a sufficient number of likely candidates, you may want to spend time developing one or two dependable customers for them in their unaltered condition. The customer might be a smith or hobbyist who wants to do the work for potential resale. By having this pre-identified customer, you can more confidently purchase these pieces and turn them quickly. That fast turn will be essential because of the predictably small mark-up you'll realize on them.

TOUCHING UP WOOD AND METAL FINISHES

Almost without exception, these repairs take more time and effort than we anticipate at first look. It would probably be prudent to limit wood touch-ups to removal of what I call "paint scuffs." These are spots where the wood has rubbed against a painted surface and the paint has come off onto the finish. Generally, a scuff can be removed by rubbing gently with solvent on a patch, or with solvent and fine steel wool. But this repair always carries with it the danger of going too far and damaging

Birchwood Casey's paste blue doesn't run like the liquid blues can, and gives excellent results. CREDIT: BROWNELLS

"44/40" is great for touching up screw ends, small finish blemishes, etc. It gives a deep black finish that is tougher than many other cold blues. CREDIT: BROWNELLS

Lin-Speed is another excellent choice, gives a fine gloss finish, and mattes out with less danger of "going white."

Tru-Oil Gun Stock finish is an easy-to-use finish that will give you great results. It can be applied with the fingers or with a folded patch. It's especially appropriate for a high-gloss finish, but it can be cut back to a "matted" result if done carefully. CREDIT: BROWNELLS

the original surface. Be very, very careful, and go slowly.

For worn spots in the finish, you may want to try a touch-up if you are absolutely positive that the finish is Tru-Oil or Linspeed. These two lend themselves to blending with the existing surface much better than most other finishes. The idea here is to touch up only the rubbed or worn spot, but the tendency is to feather out the repair too far, making it very noticeable.

With metal, you'll sometimes have the less expensive guns come in with paint spatters on them. Maybe there's something in the painting handbook that says you have to leave guns standing in the corner when using a paint roller. And, of course, you'll also encounter arachnid excreta, which resembles paint spots but is much tougher to remove. Anyhow, it happens, and when it does, try fine steel wool and solvent on the blued areas.

Sometimes the spot is noticeable after the paint comes off, but the gun still looks better. If you are very careful not to go too far, you can use a cold blue solution to darken sharp edges, worn spots on screwheads, etc. These are all tiny areas. If you use cold blue on any larger areas, it will show up at first glance. It's hard to control the spread of cold blue liquid because it is very thin, and the cream version is worse. Both forms will change the appearance of the adjacent undamaged blue, so use only very small amounts. Beyond that, leave things alone or have the whole thing refinished.

16. DETERMINING MARKET PRICE

A frequently repeated phrase throughout this book has been "market value," which we have defined as the price at which we would expect to sell the gun to the end user (someone buying it for his own use or as a gift). And one of the key requirements of making the TEK system work for you is your detailed knowledge of market values in your niche area. But how, exactly, do we determine what the market value of a particular firearm is?

To begin with, we need to understand that firearms are not like the stock market. At any point in time, anyone buying a share of Wal-Mart stock pays the same price as anyone else. The price may change later, going up or down, but it's the same for everyone at a given moment.

The gun market works somewhat differently. Whereas every share of Wal-Mart common stock is the same as every other share, each gun is different from all others, even those of the same make and model and in the same condition classification. Also, there is no centralized marketplace for guns, as there is for stocks. So what we really have is a whole series of gun markets, and the same gun may sell for a slightly different price in each of these markets.

Therefore, when we speak of the market price for a firearm, we're talking about a small range of prices within which we would expect the gun to sell, anywhere in the country.

Whenever a gun is sold to an end user, its market value has been established. When a similar gun is sold, its value is identified. As more and more of this same make and model are sold, we find that the prices cluster in a narrow band. This band represents the market value of that make and model.

Although there is no central clearinghouse for sales information, it's surprising how people in different parts of the country come to basically the same conclusion about what a gun is worth. Some of this is due to the availability of "asking price" information in online forums, in indexed gun publications, and in gun value references. And some of it, especially in the case of production guns, is calculated from the manufacturer's suggested retail price (MSRP).

When a maker introduces a new firearm, he also provides a suggested retail selling price, which basically defines where the manufacturer sees his gun in relationship to others of his make, and to those of his competitors. The gun company doesn't expect many of the guns to actually sell at the suggested price, but, for example, if the MSRP is $600, the company is telling the world that it believes this piece to be worth twice as much as its $300 entry, and about half as much as its competitor's $1,200 gun. So the MSRP won't really tell us what the market price is.

You'll find that if you decide to get an FFL, all of a sudden flyers and catalogs from the gun wholesalers in your region start showing up in your mailbox. (How do they know you're in business? They bought a mailing list of FFL addresses in their area from the government.) For guns that are still in production, or very recently so, your maximum buying price will probably be the wholesaler's price to the retailer. Since you can buy "model x" for such-and-such a price from the wholesaler, you would be foolish to pay more than that to an individual seller, no matter that he may have purchased his gun at retail. If the customary retail price in your area on this gun is 10 percent over this cost, this is your market value figure for the gun in new/as new condition.

Again, what we're actually trying to find out is the range in which the gun has been trading recently. If we look up the gun in a "gun values" book, such as *Flayderman's Guide to Antique American Firearms* (DBI Books), *Gun Trader's Guide* (Stoeger Industries), and *Standard Catalog of Firearms* (Krause Publications), we'll probably find almost all of the makes and models listed, along with a price for one or more grades of condition. Many times, these books will provide a starting point.

In periods of heavy inflation, however, the price shown in the book may be "old news" by the time the work is written, edited, published and marketed. Even the versions that are published annually are often way behind the times when prices are changing rapidly. I've found, though, that these reference books are useful in determining the "relative" value of guns. Regardless of the actual price realized in the sale, they show that, for example, a Smith Model 10 should sell for about half the price of a Model 36, or that a Remington 700B is worth about X percent more than a 700A. It's important to learn and remember these relationships, because they tend to remain relevant, even though the prices themselves may move up and down.

Another source for price information are the "gun newspapers," such as the indexed *Gun List* (Krause Publications, 700 E. State St., Iola, WI 54990) and the un-indexed *Shotgun News* (No. 2 News Plaza, Second Floor Peoria, IL 61614). The index feature is extremely useful to the gun trader for two reasons: It shows the number of available pieces of this make and model, and it provides a quick price comparison. These "offered at" prices are perhaps less valuable than would be the "actually sold at prices," but since actuals are not available in any sort of compilation, we have to make do with the next best.

Of course, not all guns are offered every week or month, and for that reason it is useful to keep a number of back issues of these papers. Here again, the index speeds up the reference process. When several successive issues do not show any pieces offered for sale, we can begin to conclude that the particular item is not readily available (or extremely unpopular). Naturally, we have to make sure that we are looking under the correct index heading. Some guns are listed in a generic section, such as military or doubles, rather than under the specific make and model in the main section, so be sure to check all the options.

We looked previously at auction catalogs and the "post-sale price sheets." This is one source of "actual" data that is very interesting, but it is usually hard to get enough sales data together over the short term to be able to really see a market.

A very important source of availability and price data that shouldn't be overlooked is the online auction services. By using the available search capabilities, you will be able to quickly review similar models and see what sort of prices are being asked for and obtained. Another advantage is that by putting these auction items on your "watch list," you will be able to see the final bid, even if you aren't watching the closing session. Realize, of course, that some of the auctions are curtailed early and the sales actually concluded offline, but even in these cases, you'll get some idea of what is available for sale.

Gunbroker.com and Auctionarms.com are two of the biggest sites, but there are numerous others, and more pop up regularly. For accessories and parts, watch eBay, but eBay doesn't allow guns or ammunition, so go to one of the less politically-correct sites for those. We'll talk more about these sites later on.

17. TEK AND THE OFFER PRICE

From one or several of the sources noted above, let's assume that we have calculated a $400 market value for the gun we are considering purchasing. How do we now decide what offer to make to the seller? Just as a reminder, the market price selected reflects condition, scarcity and demand at the retail level.

Turn again to the TEK-I table. For the sake of this example, let's say you have decided that your margin should be in the 30 percent range. You've also established a CSD point total as follows: Condition—the gun is in NRA Excellent condition (four points); Scarcity—the piece is no longer in production, but it is still seen pretty often (award two points). Demand—the configuration is something that three of your customers were looking for about two months ago. They may already have found what they needed, but the peak demand period for this gun (hunting season) is only about a month away (so give three points here).

The CSD point total equals 4 + 2 + 3, or 9 points. In the far left column of the discount table, we select the line for a gun with 7-9 points. Following that line one column to the right, we find that, in order to improve the turn potential, the gun should be offered for sale at 75 percent of market. Continue to the right on that same line until we intersect with the column for our selected margin, in this case 30 percent.

The value displayed, 53 percent of retail, is the maximum price we will offer for the gun. This translates to a dollar figure of $212. You should either come down to $210 or go up to $215. In order to give yourself some negotiating room, you may be tempted to start lower, say at $180 or $190, then come up. Be careful, though, because even at the final offering price, you will still be well below the market price. The farther below that price your offer is (the farther down and right on the discount table), the more aware you have to be of what I call "offer shock."

"Offer shock" happens when your offer is far away from what the seller had in mind. If this shock factor is too great, the seller gets upset, the whole negotiation collapses instantly, and the opportunity is lost. When you perceive that the potential for this is high, you will probably want to simply give the seller your best offer right up front, probably a straight $200. He will probably counter with, say, $300 . . . "let's split the difference."

This is when you must politely but firmly let him know that your offer is the best you can make, based on your assessment of what you can sell the gun for. Project the idea that you also realize he knows what he has to get for the gun, maybe something like this: "I can offer $215 for the gun. Now, if you tell me you can't let it go for that price, I understand completely. But $215 is the best offer I can make."

Be careful not to infer that you are paying him full retail value, or that you are doing him some sort of favor by your offer. He understands that you are buying with the intention of reselling for a profit. He accepts that, and can deal with it, provided you don't try to con him.

The temptation here may be to "round off" the offer at $225. Don't do it. Get in the habit of absolutely sticking to your offer. Otherwise, you'll be at $250 before you know what happened. At $250, your profit will be only $50, or a margin of 16.6 percent. That's barely one-half of your objective. Furthermore, if something should go wrong and you can't get the full $300, you could be looking at little more than a couple of dollars profit. Set that maximum price and don't go past it.

The attitude that you project during this negotiation is all-important. For starters, be interested in the deal and focused on the customer, but appear calm and unemotional. The seller needs to receive the message that you are very willing to purchase the gun, but you aren't desperate. This is strictly a business deal, so your best offer is your best offer, and you will not be upset with the seller if the deal doesn't happen. When the seller understands that this is your approach, he or she will tend to reflect the same businesslike and unemotional attitude, which makes it easier to move forward.

Now, we've already decided what our maximum offer will be on this gun, but what happens if the seller "sweetens the deal" by, for example, adding a few boxes of ammunition?

Watch out for the temptation to get wrapped up in this sort of "extras" deal, because your interest is the gun. Forget what the ammo is "worth" and consider what you'll find it sold for in Wal-Mart or in one of the discount catalogs. Then cut that price by 30 percent to 50 percent, and make this your selling price. Why the 30 percent-50 percent cut? You are selling pre-owned merchandise. There's no such thing as "used" ammunition (other than the brass); new is new, and this is not. Unless you know positively that you can make the same profit and turn on the ammo as you plan to make on the gun, decline the offer.

Let's take another example. The customer comes in with a Winchester Model 70 in .338 Winchester (also known as the Alaskan model). The gun appears to have just come out of the box, and in fact he has the box and the original hanging tags and papers with it. He says it belonged to his father, and as far as he knows, it wasn't ever fired. He also has a full box of ammo for it.

Examination of the face of the bolt shows no "case ring" around the primer, and there is no brass track on the magazine follower. The area where the bolt lugs bear shows virtually no wear. These observations, along with the fact that the box of ammo is full, support the idea that the gun may be unfired. Further inquiry reveals that his father planned to hunt in Alaska, but his companions backed out and he never rescheduled the trip.

After evaluating the gun as in "as new" condition, you assign it five points because it is likely to be unfired. You know that there were relatively few of the Alaskans made, but you find two offered in Gun List in the past three months, and find one on the current auction sites, so give it three points for scarcity. In your "wants" file, there are six names of people who are looking for excellent or better Winchester 70s. Looks like this one could go quickly, so award four points for demand. Notice that we probably could have added another point each for scarcity and demand, but it is better to be conservative.

The total CSD point award is 12. Going to the discount table, you find that 12 points should sell at 85 percent of retail. Moving to the 30 percent margin column, you find your maximum offer percentage to be 60 percent. After factoring in the condition, the box and tags and the unfired condition, you figure the retail price to be $1,000. This means you would sell the gun for $850, which seems to be a price that would make your collectors anxious to conclude the deal quickly. Your max offer price, therefore, would be $600. OK, how do you open the ball?

Recognize that this may be a tough buy, especially if the customer is in touch with gun values. Of course, you could just decide to pay what you have to pay up front to get the gun, then add a couple of hundred and turn it over. But when you take this approach, you are abandoning your predetermined strategy, and that will eventually get you in trouble. In this case, I would start at $600 and plan to go to possibly $650, moving the selling price up to $950. If you are positive that you can get the $1,000 from your buyer, figure your offer at 30 percent off the $1,000, or $700. In this way, you are reducing the "offer shock" without cutting into your margin.

As we said, if your seller knows what he has, and especially if there are other buyers around, you may have a hard time making this deal. Winchester Model 70s are just too well known and too highly sought after. One way to avoid the problem is to stay away from the high-profile guns . . . the Colts, Winchesters, Parkers, and such. Work with Marlins, Remingtons, Smiths, etc. They are still popular pieces, but don't have the same "high-roller" image. Later on, we'll talk about working at a riskier level, using the TEK-II tables to be successful in this tougher environment. For now, though, make the offer, and if it simply won't work for the seller, skip the deal and move on.

One point that we need to revisit here is the reason we lower the selling price as we move down the CSD scale: We are trying to increase the buyer's motivation to buy. In other words, we're giving him a better deal. This is necessary because guns with lower point values are less desirable. Those with higher point values are more desirable. We do not lower the offer price in order to make more money on the deal. We buy at a lower price with the intent to sell at a lower price. Don't get greedy after the buy and before the sale and decide to jack up the minimum selling price. Doing so will burn you on a regular basis by causing you to miss your turns target. If, in spite of this recommendation, you elect to raise the minimum sell price and still manage to hit your turns target on a regular basis, you may want to re-examine your market-price evaluations, because it would appear that they are be uniformly low. If you don't adjust your evaluations, it will eventually get in the way of your success.

USING ONLINE AUCTIONS AS A SOURCE

When you bid in an auction at one of the online sites, you'll find some advantages and some disadvantages as compared to an "in person" auction. The biggest disadvantage, as a buyer, is that the audience is potentially everyone in the world, literally, who is interested in that gun.

Since you are buying for resale using TEK, you'll do a lot of looking and bidding, but you'll actually buy only a small percentage of what you bid on. That's because the bidding audience is made up of both end users and resellers, just as you would see at a regular auction.

Another disadvantage, though a lesser one, is that you won't actually get to handle the product before you bid. You have to rely on the information and photos supplied by the seller, and while it's assumed he is making his best effort to describe the material and answer your questions, handling is still better.

The final downside to online auctions is the delay between completion of the auction and your actual receipt of the gun. And, of course, there is always the chance that something could go wrong in the transfer/transit process.

The biggest advantage is the mirror side of the biggest disadvantage. You are looking at every gun being auctioned online anywhere in the world. Sure, you may have to search a little for some of the more obscure sites, but you can find them. If you have a customer looking for something special, this wide-angle look can help. Obviously, it also allows your customer to go out and bid for the gun on his own, but so be it. Even if he wins the bid, he will still need a transfer agent, which we'll talk about later.

For me, the other advantage is the pace of the auction. During the real thing, you have to make pretty quick decisions, yet avoid getting caught up. Online, you can sit back and think about the next bid without worrying, except right at the very end, about the piece being "knocked down" by the auctioneer while you're trying to make up your mind to bid.

Virtually all of the auction sites have a "maximum bid" or "automatic bidding" capability, which works just like the live auctioneer's absentee bid. Gunbroker.com, for example, calls theirs "auto bid." This system is a great asset for the gun trader, because it allows you to simply enter the maximum bid you have determined using TEK, then go away and bid on another auction. You know that Auto Bid is watching the action and will nibble away at your maximum bid, if there are counter bids, until either you win the piece or your maximum bid is exceeded by someone else.

I am hard pressed to see any disadvantage to using this auto-bid feature because I know that it does work "as advertised." The point is, if someone wants the gun at a price higher than your best offer, he'll outbid you anyway.

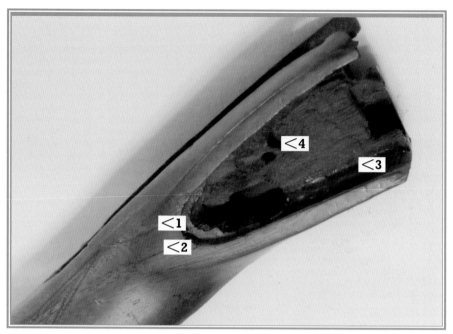

1 and 2 show obvious external stock cracks that are readily discernable. 3 points to an internal repair with glue still visible. The problem at 4 is less obvious, because a portion of the wooden "web" is missing, with only a little fresh wood to indicate it was ever there. Without disassembling the gun, the damage at 3 and 4 would not be readily apparent in your examination. TIM MARCHOK PHOTO—ALL RIGHTS RESERVED.

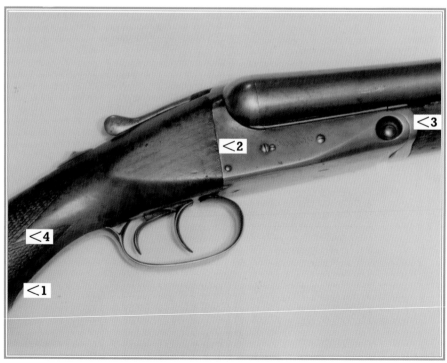

Watch for cracks at 1, 2 and 3. Notice also the filled-in checkering (4) at the wrist, indicating a probable refinish. TIM MARCHOK PHOTO—ALL RIGHTS RESERVED.

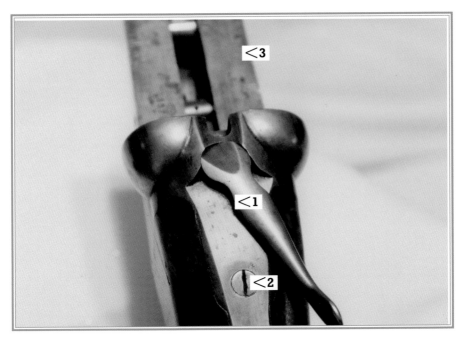

Arrows point out spots where color case may still be visible on older guns, even though most of the exterior color has faded completely. (1) and (2) show the areas protected by the top lever when in the closed position. (3) indicates the top of the frame normally covered by the rear of the barrels when the action is closed.

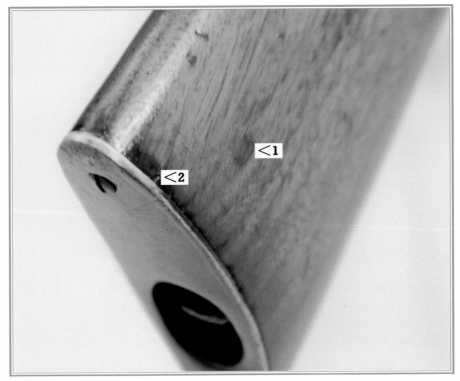

Notice the high contrast here between the fresh wood at the middle of the stock (1) and the oil/oxide-stained wood (2) next to the buttplate.

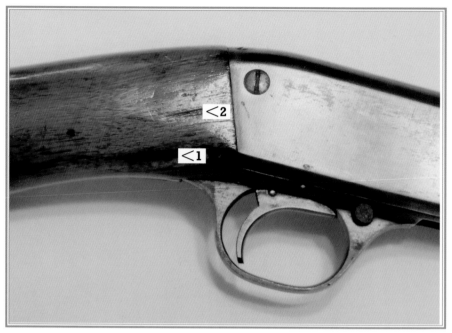

Another example of poor refinishing ... the dark stains under the finish (1), and the surface gouge with finish inside it, at (2).

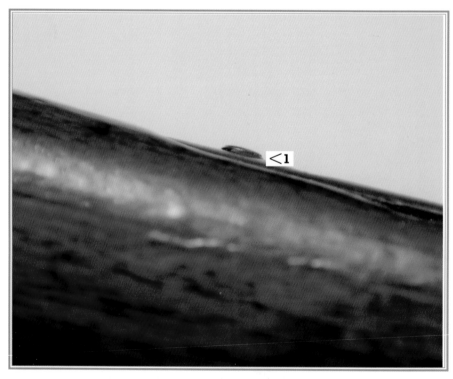

When the end of a screw protrudes from the surface like this (1), it may indicate a replacement screw, but more likely the wood separating the action tangs was sanded during a refinish, allowing the tangs to move closer together when the screw was tightened. When that occurs, the end of the screw will naturally protrude.

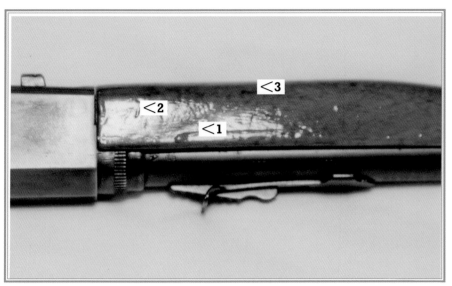

The "sag" or "run" in the polyurethane (1) used to refinish this forearm is a dead giveaway of the rework. But even without it, there are clues to be seen at 2, where the compression ding is filled with the finishing material, and at 3, showing the dark stains under the poly finish. These stains are probably the best indication of all of a re-do. TIM MARCHOK PHOTO—ALL RIGHTS RESERVED.

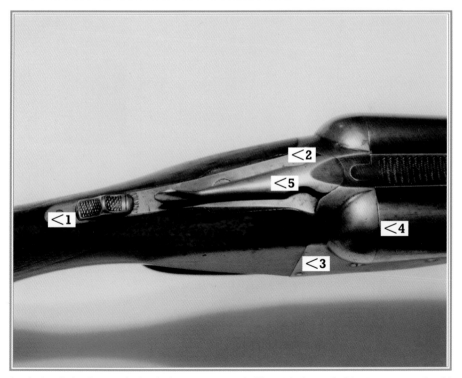

Look closely for tiny cracks beginning to sprout at 1. Also at 1, the end of the tang screw should be flush with the surface of the tang or slightly recessed. Wood should be tight to the action at 2, with no springiness. Look for checks and splits at 3. Barrels should be tight to the recoil plate at 4, with no looseness in any direction. Top lever (5) is just shy of being centered on the tang. This is better than being past center, which can indicate excessive wear on the locking surfaces.
TIM MARCHOK PHOTO—ALL RIGHTS RESERVED.

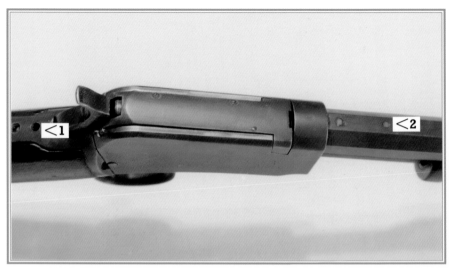

The extra holes added to this gun at 1 and 2 certainly didn't increase its value. Best solution here would be to clean the epoxy out of the holes at 2 and fill both 1 and 2 with plug screws. You'll want to "age" the screw heads to make them match up.

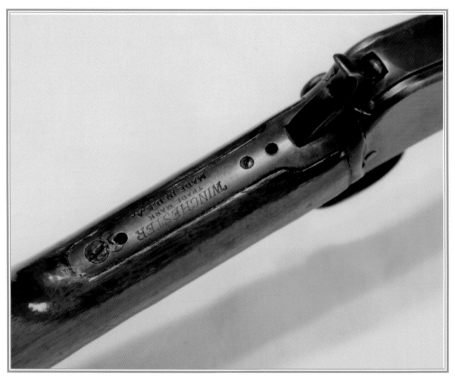

Upon encountering something like this Winchester 1890, the experienced guntrader will realize he is looking at a refinished stock, a battered tang screw and two added holes in the tang (and two more on the barrel, beyond the edge of the picture). Given all this cosmetic damage, the market for this gun will be the shooter, not the collector. Provided it functions properly, you will probably find a strong demand for the gun as long as you offer it at "shooter" price levels. The damage is sufficient that the guntrader probably won't consider restoring the gun, but rather selling it "as is." The gun would grade only "fair," at best, yet would be better sold intact instead of being "parted out."

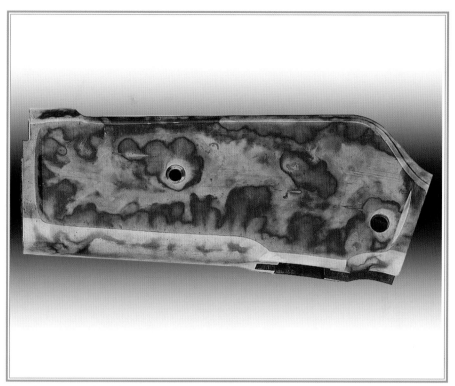

Here is an example of fine color case-hardening from Turnbull Restorations. An original still in this condition would be in great demand, given the tendency for case colors to fade over time. DOUG TURNBULL—TURNBULL RESTORATIONS 2004.

This Colt shows color case with a little less yellow and a little more blue. The results are not predictable, but all are beautiful. Here again, the small parts (loading gate, hammer, trigger, etc.) are also colored. DOUG TURNBULL—TURNBULL RESTORATIONS 2004.

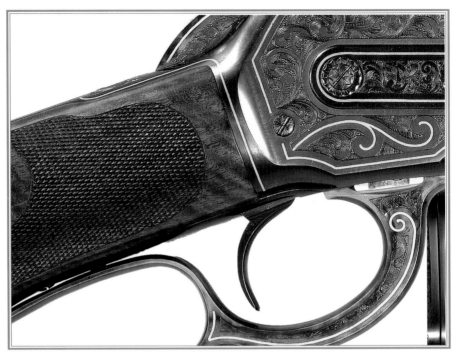

This close-up shows what virtually perfect checkering looks like. Much of what you see from the factory will not meet this standard, but the closer the better. Note the complete absence of run-outs. Here is also another example of fine wood to metal fit. DOUG TURNBULL—TURNBULL RESTORATIONS 2004.

In addition to this gorgeous receiver, note the colors on the lever and hammer. Excellent fitting of wood to metal at the rear of the receiver is also shown here. This is one of the marks of fine stockmaking. DOUG TURNBULL—TURNBULL RESTORATIONS 2004.

Here is a Colt Ace showing another beautiful restoration job. One problem the guntrader may encounter will be telling this grade of rework from a factory original job. In many cases, the factory work will not be nearly as good. A restoration of this quality will generally command at least as much in the market as the factory gun in 100 percent original condition. DOUG TURNBULL—TURNBULL RESTORATIONS 2004.

This example of a restored Remington double shows what great color case looks like, and also provides a good example of a Damascus barrel. As noted in the text, the pattern may vary from parallel lines to a rosette pattern, like the one shown. DOUG TURNBULL—TURNBULL RESTORATIONS 2004.

I've been told by some bidders that they are afraid the bid will immediately go right to their maximum. Well, if two competing auto bids are submitted, that's exactly what will happen, but it would happen anyway if the two parties were handling the bids personally. So go ahead and use these systems without worrying that they are something other than what they claim to be.

You will probably find your potential bid prospect by running a search at the site, either by a specific firearm, or by browsing price levels or "auction-stage listings," or both. Auction-stage listings may be "most recent additions" or "shortest time to closing." One very productive way to proceed is to search a specific make and model, and sort the output list by "shortest time left." For the immediate closers, definitely use auto bid to let you participate in multiple auctions simultaneously. When the closing is a week off, you have the luxury of watching it yourself, but not so when you have seven auctions closing in five minutes.

Before you bid, of course, you'll want to be sure you know what it is you are bidding on. You can rely on the seller's information, but sometimes the seller makes a mistake in the model number or in some other important fact. The vast majority of sellers are honest, and if they goof, they'll make good somehow. But once in a while you will encounter a real stinker from the schools of "caveat emptor" and "you bought it, you own it." You can use the auction service's feedback system and write the seller a nasty-gram, but that still doesn't get you what you thought you were bidding on.

So . . . if there is even a hint of a question is your mind, ask the seller for confirmation. Then, if something does go wrong, you have a leg to stand on. Also, if you need to see a picture of some area of the gun other than what's shown online, ask the seller. If he refuses, don't bid. It's that simple.

When you encounter a gun listed with a "reserve," it means that the seller has set a minimum acceptable bid, the amount of which will be hidden from you. I'm not a big fan of reserves, but they're there and we have to deal with them. Sometimes the seller will disclose the reserve to you if you send an email, and sometimes he will get all upset with you for asking. Here again, the TEK approach works well. Figure your maximum offering price, place an "auto bid" for that amount, and see what happens. If you are below the reserve, you'll get an immediate response to that effect, following which you would move on to the next item.

One caution worth mentioning is that you always want to bid with the expectation of winning. Be aware of the sum total of the bids you have made, keeping it within the size of your stake. You never know for sure when you might get lucky and win everything you have open. Remember, if you are the high bidder you are basically making a contract to buy the gun at the price you have bid. It is highly unethical to fail to honor a winning bid, even if the police won't come knocking on your door. One technique the auction sites have for combating non-payers is the feedback system. Buyer and seller have the ability to submit comments on the transaction, and as gushy as the good ones are, the bad verbiage gets downright nasty. When a non-payer can't convince the auction site that the action was justified, there is a good chance that he or she will be blocked for participating in any further auctions. I've also heard of situations where "Site A" has reacted to serious non-payment activity on "Site B" by also blocking the individual from participation at "Site A."

We previously mentioned that customer of yours who went to the auction site and bid on a gun directly, at the same time you were looking at it for him. Unless you don't expect to do business with this customer again, it's probably not a good idea to brace him on this. Rather, realize that he will need someone to receive the gun from the seller for him, since he won't have an FFL. You may want to offer to handle the transaction for him, for a tidy fee, of course. Some dealers have a sliding scale of fees, depending on the frequency of transactions.

TRADES

You won't be very far into your first day of gun trading before someone offers you a trade. Trades come in three basic flavors: I give you cash, you give me cash, or we swap straight up. Regardless of the terms, however, there is one rule of thumb covering trades: Never trade unless you are going to come out ahead. As obvious as that may seem, rookie gun traders, and even some experienced ones, often forget it. How do you come out ahead? Here are some examples of "always, never and sometimes" deals. Adjust your cost for any cash given or received with the trade.

Always make the following trades:

1. The gun I'm getting will sell for more than the one I have, and will take no longer to sell.

2. The gun I'm getting will sell for the same price as mine, but will sell faster.

Don't make the following trades:

1. The gun I'm getting will sell for the same price as mine, but will take longer to sell.

2. I'm getting two (or more) guns for my gun. In total, the selling price and turn time will be the same as for mine. (This will require more sell transactions for the same return.)

Make the following trades only if the numbers are right:

1. The gun I'm getting will sell for more than mine, although it will take longer to sell.

2. I'm getting multiple guns for mine. All meet my CSD criteria. In total, the selling price will be higher, but the sell time will be longer (or vice versa). Your calculations should include the fact that you will spend added effort to sell the additional guns, even if the price and turn time are better.

FIGURING THE COST OF A TRADED GUN

Whether your trade is straight up or involves a cash "give or get," you will always be better off if you treat a trade as two separate transactions . . . a purchase and a sale. This approach allows you to examine both aspects for acceptability. If either doesn't measure up, pass on the trade. Look at this simple example:

I purchase a shotgun for $150 and put it up for sale at $225. A customer offers to give me his rifle, plus $50 cash (old-time horse traders used to call this the "boot") for my gun. Since the $225 selling price for my gun was my idea, it naturally meets my criteria. But if we consider this deal as two transactions, how much are we paying for the rifle? Do we subtract the $50 "boot" from the original cost of the shotgun, or from the selling price of the shotgun? The answer is, we always think as though the buyer had handed us the full price of our gun, and then we turned around and gave him that much right back for his, less "the boot." In this case, he bought my gun for $225 . . . great. Now I'm buying his gun for $175. Is that a good deal? Only if I would have offered him at least $175 to buy the gun outright.

Be careful not to fall into the trap of thinking about his rifle costing us only $100 (the original outlay for the shotgun minus the $50 boot). Otherwise, you could easily spend your time swapping guns and have little or no profit to show for it. For instance, if you went this route, you would now say that the rifle he traded to me cost only $100, so it should be priced at $150, the same margin as I had on the shotgun. When I sell it, my net profit on the entire package will be only $50, even though I did the selling work twice: I paid $150 for the original shotgun and wound up, after the rifle sold, with $150 plus the $50 boot. This is $25 less profit than I would have had if I had simply sold the shotgun outright, and I only would have had to sell one gun. ■

NOTES

MAXIMIZE YOUR SALE...

SUCCESSFUL
SELLING

Now we have arrived at a point where you have one or more firearms, purchased using the TEK system, ready for resale. How do we proceed? Before we explore selling techniques, let's take a brief look at how we are allowed to proceed, as in legally.

Previously, we've used the term firearm to cover any form of shooting appliance, without regard to size or age. Legally, however, firearm has a very specific definition. At the Federal level, it excludes, as antiques, anything manufactured prior to 1898. Not that the model itself was made before 1898, but that the physical specimen in hand goes back that far. If you are going to treat a gun as an antique, be sure that you have dated it correctly. Federal law also treats as non-firearms most muzzle-loaders and air guns, regardless of their age. State laws sometimes mirror Federal definitions, but New York, for instance, insists that a handgun, no matter when it was made, is a modern arm (and so subject to licensing) if it uses ammunition available "in the normal course of trade."

What are we allowed to do, and how do we do it in today's legal environment? To begin with, I'm assuming that you are an honest individual, and one who has neither the intent to violate the law, nor any desire to do so inadvertently. Start with the understanding that firearms are controlled at Federal, state and local levels by a number of different laws, each having its own scope and application, and some of which even contradict one another. Federal laws apply across the entire nation, but they often do not come into play until the activity crosses state lines. State and local laws stop at the border of the state or locality, but will override Federal law if the state or local law is the more restrictive. Within an area of jurisdiction, the most restrictive law will always apply.

The bases for most elements of firearms control at the national level are the National Firearms Act (1934) and the Gun Control Act (1968).

The National Firearms Act establishes controls on certain types of firearms and accessories (fully automatic arms, silencers, short-barreled arms, etc.), provides for their registration, and regulates their transfer. Guns covered by this law are generically known as "NFA guns."

The Gun Control Act imposed a wide array of restrictions on the ownership and transfer of firearms, and provided for a licensing system (Federal Firearms License/Curio and Relics License) to control the flow of firearms across state lines.

18. THE FEDERAL FIREARMS LICENSE

If you are going to be a gun trader, obtain a Federal Firearms License. You may not agree with the law, but you are going to have to work within the framework of the law to make money as a gun trader. Working legally, but without an FFL, restricts your options far too much.

There is some confusion about what a Federal Firearms License (FFL) allows the holder to do. Quite simply, an FFL allows an individual ("licensee") to receive firearms across state lines ("in interstate commerce"), and that's all it does. It doesn't allow you to carry concealed weapons around the country. It doesn't permit you to have a fully automatic arm in a state that doesn't allow them. It won't let you conduct a business in an area where that business would violate zoning laws.

An FFL is available to, and is required of, any individual intending to engage in the business of selling firearms to non-licensees residing in a state other than his own. There is an ongoing debate about the definition of "engaging in the business." A person selling one gun in a year is probably not engaging in the business, while a person who sells a few dozen guns probably is. The key appears to be in the person's intent, along with the repetitive nature of the sales. For example, if a person is liquidating his collection of 1,000 guns, he is not engaging in the business because he is selling personal property, and once it is gone, he will stop selling. Some folks who want to avoid the licensing requirement claim they are buying for their collection, and selling from their collection. BATF personnel are rarely misled by this scam.

As a gun trader, you will be both buying and selling firearms. An FFL will make your life easier by far. Without one, you are restricted to selling to either residents of your own state who are permitted to own a firearm, or to FFL holders in other states (who are probably buying for resale), or to CRL holders in other states (who are limited in what they can buy). The question always asked here is, "But if I don't have an FFL, I can't run a background check, so how do I know that the person buying from me is permitted to have a firearm?" The answer is that you don't know, and that's where your risk is . . . you are the seller, and the seller is responsible for the sale, not the buyer.

If, for example, you sell to a felon, you could be liable to prosecution, even if he told you he wasn't a felon. If you are going to sell without an FFL, and therefore without a background check, at least make sure that the person shows identification establishing that he is a resident of your state. Keep a copy of that identification, and have him sign a statement to the effect that he is not prohibited from receiving a firearm. This will at least establish your intent to keep everything legal.

People considering getting into the gun trading game sometimes hesitate because of the licensing requirement. They are concerned that the government will know too much about them, or will step in and take away their guns. Well, gun control is an unfortunate fact of life, so get over it, and rest assured that they will not learn any more about you from your FFL application than they already know . . . which is everything.

There is no reason why an FFL will be denied to you, provided you have a clean record and your intended place of business (home, storefront, wherever) conforms to local zoning codes. The license is issued for conducting a business, so if your only objective is to buy guns cheaply for yourself, you aren't really operating a business. BATF usually will want to see that you have hours when you are "open to the public." If zoning does not permit that, you may have some scrambling to do. With the advent of Internet auction sites and e-commerce, the requirement for public access may receive less emphasis in the future, because one can certainly transact a lot of business online without ever setting eyes on your buyers. Of course, your sales would all have to go out by way of an FFL at the receiving end.

If you have been convicted of something, it will undoubtedly slow down the application process, but it doesn't necessarily mean you'll be denied . . . unless you have been convicted of a crime for which the judge could have sentenced you to more than 12 months in prison (whether he actually did or not). In that case, don't even bother to apply. You are already prohibited from possessing a firearm.

If you are upset over governmental gun control, operating a business without a license is NOT the way to change things. Work through your elected representatives and through the NRA, NSSF, etc. The initial cost of the FFL, at this writing, is $200, with a renewal every three years at $90.

Once the FFL is issued, the only "burden" it carries is the requirement for keeping certain records. You will have to record, in a "bound book," your firearm acquisitions and disposals. If you are doing enough volume to justify it, you may want to consider applying for permission to use one of the approved electronic "bound book" systems. You will also have to have every non-FFL buyer complete a form 4473 and usually you'll have to call in the information on that form to the FBI for a background check.

Occasionally, you may receive a visit from a BATF inspector, who will ask to see your records and will compare your inventory to your paperwork. This happens infrequently, and the inspectors are generally gracious and courteous people.

CURIO AND RELICS LICENSE

Think of a C&R License as FFL-Lite. It applies to firearms more than 50 years old and allows interstate receipt. The record-keeping is similar to that of an FFL, but the CRL cannot sell to non-licensees out of state. It is essentially a collecting license, and not really intended for operating a business. You can find out more about the "cans and can'ts" of a C&R license from the BATF website.

19. BUYING WITH AN FFL

FFLs are issued in a number of different types, depending on what the individual wants to do: importing/exporting, selling, or manufacturing. Purchases from outside the U.S. may require an import FFL. Full auto arms require a full auto FFL. When you hold a dealer FFL, you can purchase a firearm from anyone who legally owns the gun, living anywhere in the U.S.

How do you know that the gun is legally owned? For starters, if a license to possess is required by his state or locality of residence, he should have one. Beyond that, the best way to demonstrate that you are trying to purchase only legally owned arms is to require the seller to sign a statement to the effect that he is the legal owner or the owner's legal agent. Does this guarantee he won't lie? Of course not. But if it turns out the guns were not legally owned, at least you will be able to show what lawyers call "due diligence" in the matter. Naturally, should you have any suspicion that something is amiss with a potential transaction, run away from it.

Taking this approach will mean that purchases in the aisles of a gun show, or from some "guy on the street," may not be a good idea because often times these sellers don't like to give a last name.

Although in many places rifles, shotguns and pistols are treated alike as firearms, some states license handguns separately, or require that all arms be registered. So, let's suppose that a seller approaches you and says, as will happen, "I have a pistol I'd like to sell, but I don't have a license for it." Your immediate two-part response must be (1) "I can't touch the gun unless it is legally owned, but there may be a way to make it legal," and (2) "What sort of pistol is it?" By responding in that order, you establish your intent to comply with the law, just in case the seller has a badge out of sight somewhere. The second part of the response gives you an opportunity to decide whether you want to get involved with making the gun "righteous."

Whether or not this gun can become a legally owned arm depends on state and local law. Most jurisdictions have a provision somewhere that permits an individual to voluntarily surrender an illegally possessed firearm without penalty. This allows the owner to get out from under the weight of the law, but does nothing for you as the potential buyer. Many places also have regulations on the books that provide for such a gun to be held in safekeeping by the local police while a license is applied for, or while arrangements are made for transfer to a licensed party. If the transaction before you is covered by this sort of safekeeping arrangement, and if the gun is something in which you are interested, then follow the procedures in place with your local law-enforcement agency to arrange for the transfer.

If you purchase a firearm from another FFL holder, you will have to provide him with a signed copy of your FFL for his records. He is not required by law to provide you with a copy of his, but it is customary for FFLs to "exchange licenses."

There is, as of this writing at least, no requirement in BATF regulations that shipments by common carrier (UPS, etc.) go "from a dealer, to a dealer." The requirement of law is only that the transfer be going "to a dealer." This means that, legally, an owner in another state does not have to ship through his local dealer in order to get a firearm to you. However, some of the common carriers and the U.S. Postal Service require that any guns sent through them come from a dealer. I suspect that this requirement was put in place because they understand that when the package comes from a dealer, the sender will take care to be sure that it is actually going to a dealer as well. So how does UPS or the Postal Service know what's in the box? They don't, but should there be a loss, they won't honor the insurance. And in the case of the Post Office, should there be a "discovery," they might refer it to another government agency for "disciplinary action."

20. SELLING WITH AN FFL

As a holder of an FFL, you may sell to anyone in the country who is permitted to own a firearm, as long as the sale is legal in both your state and in the state of the buyer, and as long as the transfer takes place at your place of business. For example, if your customer lives in a state like New Jersey, which requires every gun buyer to hold a Firearms Identification Card, he or she would be required to present that card to you, to demonstrate that the sale complies with the laws of both states. Likewise, it would be illegal for a resident of New York to purchase a fully automatic firearm from a Class III dealer in Pennsylvania, because New York does not permit the ownership of full auto items.

Of course, you may transfer to another FFL anywhere in the country, as long as the receiving state allows the item. California, for example, has some interesting laws on this subject which apparently made sense to a majority of the legislature.

When transferring to a non-licensee, regardless of his state of residence, he must complete a Form 4473. He provides a number of items of identification, as well as answers regarding any prior criminal activity, and indicates his place of citizenship. Naturally, if he answers the "yes" questions with "no," or vice versa, the whole transaction stops right then.

He will also have to provide some form of identification, the numbers of which are recorded. After the form is completed and signed, the FFL holder contacts the FBI background check office for a "go/no-go" on the sale. If a "go," the sale moves ahead. If a "wait" or "no-go" is received, the transaction will be held up accordingly.

In the event of a "wait" or "no-go," you, as the seller, will not be told the nature of the problem. That's okay, because you won't have to spend time listening to the customer explain why it wasn't his fault. By now, the background check system has been operating long enough that people who are regularly "waited," and then cleared, are used to it and most will tell you beforehand, "I always get a delay and then a proceed."

The problem is that when very common names, like John Smith, are checked in the records, there will almost certainly be a match. The FBI has to do further checking, like birth date, social security number, place of birth, etc., to tell the good guy from the bad guy. Incidentally, the FBI is prohibited from flagging someone as having been "cleared." While it would make purchase transactions easier for common names, it also has the potential for creating a record of firearms owners. This was something the framers of the legislation wished to avoid.

It is true that complying with all of the rules takes a certain amount of time, but it is not overly burdensome. Despite that, some might be tempted to bypass the rules and purchase or sell "off paper." If you sell at gun shows, you may be asked by occasional customers "does that gun come with a pedigree?" Translation: "Is that gun recorded in your bound book, and can I buy it without completing a form 4473?"

There are two excellent reasons why you do not want to get anywhere near this type of transaction. First, it's illegal. You will sleep more soundly at night if you don't have a little voice inside wondering if you are going to hear about that gun on the six o'clock news. Secondly, there is always a chance, and in some areas a good chance, that the question is coming from an undercover officer, either as part of his assignment, or working on his own initiative. Remember that these people might sometime have to face something you sold "off paper." And entrapment doesn't come into play here, in my opinion. You, as the seller, have complete control of the situation, and no one can push you into an illegal sale. Be assured that as a licensed dealer, you will quickly develop a reputation with your local law-enforcement people, though you may be completely unaware of it. They will put you down in their book as someone who watches the law as closely as they do, or they will conclude that they need to check up on you every so often.

21. FINDING BUYERS

Good news: There are a lot of people out there who want to buy the guns that you have in your inventory. More good news: Because of the way you purchased that inventory, you are going to be able to price the guns attractively, yet still make your profit.

The first order of business in selling firearms is letting all those potential buyers know that you have them for sale. This lack of awareness is the bane of any seller. While it may always be true that there will be someone nearby who has no idea that you and your business are there, you want to make sure that this guy is the local idiot, and not a potential customer. There are a lot of people in the world who are not at all interested in firearms, and some who are avidly anti-gun. Any effort directed at selling to these people is a waste of time and money.

On the other hand, there is a group of folks who eat, breathe and drink firearms at every opportunity. We especially like these people, and their not-so-rabid fellow hobbyists, because they are our bread and butter. We also know that they talk to one another, for better or worse, so we want to be sure we take proper care of them. At least some of these people have to become aware of our existence.

If you are operating from a storefront, the awareness issue is less likely to come into play, if only because you have a large sign out front and are probably listed in the local yellow pages. If, on the other hand, your zoning does not allow signage, perhaps because you're working from a home location, you'll need to get the word out in other ways.

22. ADVERTISING

If you do enough local advertising, there is a good chance that the gun people in your area will become aware of you. Unfortunately, you usually pay for local advertising based on the number of readers, or viewers, or mailboxes reached, and these will include lots of people who aren't potential customers. In some areas, this means a majority of those reached.

One way to make the best of this situation is to limit advertising to an entry in the classifieds section, indicating that you are selling and buying. Keep the ad small and run it continuously. The constant presence is even more important than the text itself. Most papers offer a reduced rate for a long-term commitment on your part, so consider signing up for several months at a time. Do the "freebie" papers do as good a job as the subscription ones? I don't know for certain, but I lean toward the idea that if you are paying for the paper, you are more apt to read it before using it to wrap the garbage.

LOCAL ORGANIZATIONS

Every gun club, sportsmen's club, police department, highway department, etc., in the area should be aware of your existence because the members of these groups are often gun people. Send a letter, drop off a card, or perhaps take out an ad in their publication. Let them know you're there. If they run a raffle with one or more guns as the prize(s), offer to handle the buying and transfers at no charge. Go out of your way to create a favorable impression with them.

LOCAL BUSINESSES

For the same reasons, every hardware store, sports shop, gunsmith, pet supply house, etc., should know about you. Even if they are potential competitors, you may be able to work with one another to mutual advantage.

SPECIALIZED PUBLICATIONS

The advantage of specialized publications, such as Shotgun News and Gun List, is that 100 percent of their readership is at least somewhat interested in your material. Rates are relatively compatible, on an "interested-persons-reached" basis, with local papers.

You can advertise from two perspectives in these papers. First, you can limit ads to those telling people you are in the buy/sell business. This may bring you physical traffic if you are located in a well-populated area. Secondly, you can list specific pieces for sale. The downside here is in the fact that copy must be submitted well in advance of publication. If you sell the gun before it is advertised, you've basically wasted your money. If you hold it until the paper hits the street, you reduce your turn opportunities.

23. GUN SHOWS

As an FFL holder, you are allowed to sell, and of course buy, at any organized gun show held in your state of residence. The show site is considered an extension of your place of business. Unfortunately, that precludes selling at shows in neighboring states, no matter how close they are. If you live close to three adjacent states, as I do, you miss out on a lot of opportunities. Some dealers make the best of this situation by "displaying" at shows in adjacent states, but making the actual transfer back at their home base. This is perfectly legal, because under FFL regulations, it is the place of transfer that matters.

Gun shows are a great way to meet customers, but they are not always a great way to sell guns. I can't speak for all shows in all areas, but in the northeast, 100 show attendees will break out about as follows:

Ten will be serious collectors. They know exactly what they want, are looking for that alone, and are interested in absolutely nothing else. Thirty-three will be at the show because otherwise they would be doing yard work. Twenty will be open to possible purchases "if the price is right." Ten will have their own guns with them, trying to sell them to anyone who will pay top dollar. Ten will be looking for something for next season, even though last season ended only a month before. The remainder will be there to look at the guns, and to show them to their spouses, friends, or kids.

If you haven't sold at a show before, the activity usually goes something like this:

Friday night . . . a fine opportunity to move material to other dealers. The advantage of the TEK system is that it "leaves room for others" in many cases.

Saturday . . . serious collectors are there in line before the doors open. They move through the show with a purpose, stopping only when they see something on their tightly focused "want list." They make one careful pass through the show, and they are gone—probably to the next show on their list. The good part about these customers is that if you have what they want, they're ready to do business. Before the doors open on Saturday, you'll also hear from the dealers who didn't wait around after they set up on Friday night. This is another chance to move goods quickly. The remainder of the day will find the best opportunities for selling from about 10 a.m. to 2 p.m. After that, most of the folks are "looking."

Sunday . . . traffic is much lighter, unless the weather turns rainy. I think a lot of guys make deals with their other halves about gun shows on Sunday. "I'll go to services with you, then you go to the gun show with me." In any event, there always seem to be many more lookers than buyers on Sunday.

The good news about gun shows is that you'll have a lot of people looking at your offerings. The show promoter's job is to get people into the venue. Once they're in front of your table, your job is to sell to them.

Customers often come to shows with a couple of expectations. First, they believe that prices will be at least as high at the show as they would be at any store in the area. Secondly, they seem to feel that they have a moral obligation to haggle over prices.

Some of this is the fault of the guys behind the tables. Many times they do put a higher than normal "starting" price tag on the gun, reasoning that after the haggling, they will be down where they need to be. The whole thing becomes a self-fulfilling prophecy. I've been on both sides of the table at gun shows for many years, and I still have a tendency to believe what the tag says. If it says $400, my reaction is that the seller expects to wind up at some place fairly near $400 before he lets the gun sell. I certainly don't expect to see that tag if he would really be willing to sell for $250. Now if the market price for the gun should be around $250, we're not even going to get discussions started, because I would perceive us to be way too far apart.

I take the same approach when I'm behind the table. I might add $10 or $20 to give at least a little room for bargaining, but that's it. I tell potential buyers, "I don't believe in inflating the price tags just so we can come back down to this price." Interestingly, most customers respect that approach. They know that they are looking at the prices I expect to sell for, and they are either interested or they aren't. One other way this seems to work for me is that my prices start out being lower than those of my competitors at the other tables. This can create a favorable impression with potential buyers, and I've had them tell me that.

I've given up trying to figure out exactly what will sell at any given show. This month it might be .410 shotguns, the next month everyone will want Winchester lever guns, or Smith & Wesson auto-loaders. I haven't been able to relate this to seasons, or the local economy, or to moon phases. So I simply resign myself to taking everything with me, and putting what I think will be in less demand under the table, just in case. You cannot sell it to the customer at a show if it is back at the house or shop. True, they may stop by later in the week, but they may also forget all about it.

You'll notice at every show that some dealers don't seem to be at all happy to be there. They just sit behind the table, wait for the buyer to start the ball rolling, and almost appear bothered when the customer asks a question. You'll also probably notice that these guys sell a lot less than do some of the other dealers.

The flip side is the dealer who manages to speak to nearly every person who passes his table. He's on his feet constantly, meeting and greeting for all he's worth. He asks every passerby, "Is the gun in that case for sale?" And if a potential buyer shows any interest at all in something on the table, he works hard to make the sale. He treats the customer with respect, never demeaning the quality of the piece being offered, and never insulting the customer because of the asking price.

If you are blessed by having one of these folks as a neighbor dealer, and I have been, you'll also find them, almost without exception, to be possessed of an extremely broad knowledge of guns and gun prices. They are usually very unselfish, but never pushy, about sharing that knowledge with you. The only disadvantage is that I almost always seem to have these folks on the "upstream" side of the traffic flow, meaning that they get first crack at the "for sale" material coming down the aisle. It's always fun, though, to watch how they approach the buy decision. In fact, I'm sure they use something similar to our TEK system, because they almost always come to the same offer price as I would.

One of my regular neighbor dealers uses what he calls "the Rule of I Know" when he ventures outside his "knowledge niche." He buys for a price at which "I Know" I can make a profit. Still, I've watched him struggle to sell something he wasn't familiar with, even at a low price. Once again, stay inside your knowledge niche. Push hard to expand it as far and fast as you can, but always stay within it.

You'll find two sorts of people bringing pieces to a gun show to sell. First, there are those who expect, or at least want, to bring in a gun and sell it to a dealer for the top price listed in their "gun values" book. They don't really care whether they sell it or not, but if someone is willing to go to their price, great. Often they'll have a flag stuck in the muzzle indicating their asking price. Often they'll be seen leaving the show with the gun and tag intact, grumbling about dealers who "want to buy stuff for nothing."

The second sort of person has brought his gun to sell it or trade it. He understands that most of the people behind the tables are buying for resale, and that price books start going out of date before the ink is completely dry. This is a person you can perhaps do business with.

How do we start the buying process? The first trick is to get to him before he sells the gun to someone else. It's very interesting to watch dealers maneuvering for first crack at new material walking in the front door of the show. The tables dead-center at that spot are considered premium locations, and are handed down from parent to child (well, maybe not quite, but almost).

At most locations, the person can turn left or right from that center spot, and the tables just outside dead-center do all sorts of things to get the seller to turn their way. At one of the shows I do regularly, I am blessed with an "upstream" neighbor who is a complete pro, not only in terms of dealing with his customers, but especially at concentrating on getting to the incoming guns. Picture the following . . .

A gorgeous young lady with centerfold qualifications walks up to his table. At the same time, a man enters the show with a little Sharps pepperbox pistol tucked into his belt, leaving only the grip visible. The young lady whips open her blouse, revealing her assets in all their glory. My friend's response would most certainly be, "Would you mind moving to the side, dear, I'm trying to get the attention of that guy over there with the Sharps in his belt." Such is his intensity, truly refined to an enviable degree.

So let's suppose the seller does turn your way, and still has the gun with him when he arrives. For starters, ask him if the gun is for sale, if he hasn't already told you that it is. Sounds simple, but you'd be surprised how often each party waits for the other to open the dance.

Ask to look at the gun, then treat it just as carefully as you would one of your own. Handle a long gun by the stock, keeping you fingers off the metal as much as possible. I know a few dealers who put on white cotton gloves when they handle any customer's gun. That may sound like overkill, but you cannot believe what a favorable impression it creates with the customer. If you work the action, be gentle. When you check the bore with a bore-light, be careful not to bang the butt of the gun against the table. All of this care projects an image of respect and the customer will always react positively.

If, after the inspection, you are still interested in a possible purchase, ask the customer directly what his asking price is. He may have one price in mind, but give you a higher figure. Or he may ask you what you would offer.

I know some dealers who get extremely upset when the seller won't put a stake in the ground by stating what he wants, but this shouldn't be a problem. You have already figured out what your maximum offer will be, remember? If there is a lot a material going by the table, and you don't want to miss any of it, give him your best shot right up front. If he says no, thank him for showing you the gun and move on. If things are slow and you want to start negotiations a bit (and only a bit) below your limit, fine. But never, ever, try to low-ball the customer by offering a silly price just to see whether he has an idea of the worth of the gun. You will most likely only succeed in insulting him and eliminate any chance to make the purchase. If you reach your limit, and he wants to go higher, explain very frankly, "I know how much I can pay for it. If you have to get more than that, I understand completely."

24. INTERNET AUCTIONS

What we said about buying on the Internet is also applicable to selling on the Internet. Online auction sites provide you with a very large audience of bidders, as you will notice from the number of "hits" or views that your auction gets. In spite of this eager and willing audience, though, there are still a few things you can do to improve your chances of making the sale.

Most of the sites have similar fee structures, but there are usually some differences, so be sure you understand how yours works. The site will generally have a tutorial available for new buyers and sellers. Most follow the rule that the buyer pays only the bid price plus shipping. The seller usually pays a small fee for listing the gun on the site. In addition, if the gun is sold, the site will take a small "cut" of the selling price for their services. This is almost always figured on a sliding scale. You pay for these services by establishing an account with the site, with the option of giving them a credit card number to cover the fees. Otherwise, you will be expected to clear the account balance each month. (If you elect this "card" option, you might want to consider using a dedicated card with a low limit for your Internet sales fees.)

Most sites don't charge for a re-listing if the item didn't sell the last time.

There are usually listing options available, such as counters (how many hits), special placement and such, and there is often a small fixed fee for them. At a minimum, you will want a counter to see how much interest there is in the auction.

Pictures, especially good ones, are worth far more than the proverbial thousand words. Photos are used so often on these sites that auctions without them actually stand out. There may be some items that would not sell better with a picture, but guns are absolutely not one of them. So plan to submit several photos for your auction. Most sites provide for inserting at least one photo at no charge, and some permit four or five before triggering a small additional per-photo fee.

A digital camera is probably the best way to get the photos you need, though you could also use a scanner to handle other types of pictures. The digital lets you transfer pictures directly to the site, and you can store them on a diskette. The review feature on the digital camera is extremely useful, as it allows you to see what you have before taking the set-up apart. Decide what details you want to show on the gun, and be sure to focus closely on those details. Try to show any problems the gun may have. This will actually improve the bidding by letting the potential buyer be more confident that nothing is being hidden from him. Use proper lighting and background to insure a clear picture, and if you have trouble getting detail on the "here's the whole gun" shot, try taking several overlapping shots at a shorter distance.

Give all of the information you can about the gun—not just make and model, but also an explanation of any functional or cosmetic problems. When describing condition, err on the low side. I'd much rather have glowing positive feedback than mildly critical feedback. I make it a point to state in the description that I generally under-rate on condition. And by all means, add a little sales pitch. Suggest possible uses, such as "great little squirrel gun," or "handy foul weather rifle." And always offer more photos of any area on the gun that a bidder would like to see. I feared bidders would ask me for a lot of extra pix when I began using online auctions, but that doesn't seem to happen.

In addition to descriptions and data about the gun, you'll also save a lot of email time and avoid surprises if you include, at the end of your listing, what I call "boilerplate," spelling out exactly whether I accept business and personal checks or only money orders, how the shipping charges are figured, whether I need an FFL for the item, etc. Most auction sites give you an opportunity to include this info by clicking on some line items during the listing set-up, but the "site-generated" data doesn't get into your description. It is listed elsewhere, and the buyer should see it, but many times he'll blow right past it. Then you get an email, or an "I didn't know that when I bid." So make up a short paragraph or two containing the particulars of how you do business, and simply paste it to the end of every listing you create.

Communication with bidders and potential bidders during the auction is critical to success. I try to be absolutely sure that all mail is answered within 24 hours. When you respond, answer the question asked, and try to anticipate further questions your response might raise. Addressing them up front will create a favorable impression with the potential buyer.

Your auction will be scheduled to run for a specific period of time, for example, seven days. It's a good idea to schedule the end of the auction for an hour and day when you can pay close attention to any questions coming in via email. The answers you give may mean higher bids.

Sooner or later, you'll have someone ask you to accept an offer higher than the bid you currently have, and to end the auction now. You have the right, of course, to end an auction early, but there is much to be said for not doing so. The most obvious point in favor of letting the sale run to the end is that the price may well go up. The buyer is offering to pay a little more now, hoping to avoid possibly paying a lot more if the auction runs full session. If you feel that the bidding has truly maxed out, do what you think best. Remember, though, that many interested buyers wait until the last couple of hours to bid, just as bidders at a live auction wait until just before knockdown to jump in.

Once the auction closes, you and the buyer need to make contact by email or phone to arrange for payment and for any necessary FFL copy. Remember, whether you have an FFL or not, if you are shipping the gun rather than transferring it at your place of business, you may only ship it to an FFL. Here again I use a piece of "boilerplate," congratulating the winner and requesting the zip code of the FFL to which shipment will be made. Having the zip lets me figure the shipping cost, which I then email to the buyer.

The standard expectation with these online auctions is that funds and paperwork will arrive within seven to ten days. Most buyers react much more quickly, and I generally see the funds within five days. Once the money and license are in hand, you have an obligation to pack the gun well and ship it promptly. If you ship on specific days of the week, say, Tuesdays and Fridays, include that in your boilerplate.

Handgun packing is pretty straightforward. If you use USPS Priority Mail, and you'll probably find that the least expensive method, use the boxes the Post Office provides. Or get something from the local grocer.

Make sure the gun is unloaded before you pack it. (I know, but you'd be surprised.) Don't have ammo in the same package with the gun. It's illegal, and under the wrong circumstances it could lead to a bad situation, as for example, if the package goes astray. Wrap the gun securely in bubble wrap, or in about a dozen sheets of newspaper, and secure this with tape. Then fill the remaining space in the box with crumpled up newspaper. A ball of newspaper can absorb a lot of shock in a package. Or, you can use packing "peanuts" if you have them.

For long guns, you need to find a box longer than the gun itself. You can buy gun boxes from the supply houses, but that will run shipping costs up sharply. An alternative is to try your local florist. Cut flowers come in boxes long enough to fit most guns, although you may have to cut down the sides. Many shops give the boxes away. If the shop gives you the boxes, make sure they also get your flower business. One word of caution, based on experience: When you figure the shipping weight in order to tell the customer how much money to send, be sure to add in the weight of the packaging as well.

Seal and tape the box. Use a mailing label or write directly on the box itself. Include the names and addresses of both the sender and receiver. If the name includes references to a gun shop, sports shop, etc., omit that part. For example, instead of writing "Bob Smith's Gun Shop," address the box to "Bob Smith Co." Also, even though you will have to declare the contents of the package as a firearm to the carrier, don't write anything on the package to that effect. Cover the address label with clear tape to protect it from getting smudged or erased in the course of handling or by wet weather.

Many auction sellers will insure their shipments only if the buyer elects to pay for it, but I recommend you insure the package regardless of who pays. Should the package get lost, if you paid for the insurance, you get the reimbursement.

How much insurance is enough? Well, you've probably heard stories about the $30 item shipped with $5,000 of insurance and, luckily, it was lost. Therefore, the sender was $4,970 to the good. Wrong. The insurance will only cover up to the value of the item shipped, no matter how much extra insurance was purchased, so don't get carried away. Loss of the package is unlikely, anyway, so on average, you are okay with less than full coverage.

Some carriers will ask to see the FFL of the addressee; some will take your word for it. The Post Office will insist that you complete an affidavit attesting that the addressee is permitted to receive the gun, and will keep a copy of the addressee's FFL for their records.

A nice final touch is to send an email to the buyer, advising him of the ship date, the method of shipping, and the tracking number if there is one. Thank him for bidding, let him know you will post positive feedback, and ask him to do the same if he is happy with the way things went. This feedback is good to have, so ask for it instead of just waiting for it to happen . . . maybe. ■

NOTES

LEARNING THE KEY ELEMENTS OF THE TRADE...

FINER POINTS

25. GETTING INTO PARTS

As you search for guns to purchase, you are going to find a large number of pieces that fall into the categories of "junkers" and "decorators." Junkers are guns that are missing major parts, or are in such poor condition that repair, either by you or by a customer, is impossible or economically unfeasible.

A "decorator" is simply a junker that looks good on the outside, but isn't complete enough to restore. You might find that "decorators" have one good side and one bad side. There may be a market for these as "wall hangers"—guns intended to be hung over the fireplace, on the wall, or as part of some other display. You can often get away with repairs made for appearances only when dealing with a "decorator." For example, it would be fine to replace a missing external hammer on a shotgun with something that doesn't function, but looks like it might. Of course, be sure that you let the buyer know the nature of such work.

If you live near an urban area, you may connect with the local market by contacting area antique shops or interior designers for referrals. Understand that lots of these folks may abhor the general lot of guns, but can make themselves work with an old musket. Prices will be quite low, so buy accordingly and turn them quickly. Unless you are dealing with a true antique, remember that firearms in poor condition are still firearms, and all of the laws still apply, as ridiculous as that may seem when you are holding a total junker in your hand.

The remainder of the guns in this group will be "parts guns," and you will need to make a basic decision right up front on "parts guns." Their only utility is to be "parted out"; that is, to be completely disassembled and sold piece by piece. As with most things in life, gun parts are neither all good news nor bad.

The bad news is that there are an awful, awful lot of different gun parts in the world. Some are in high demand, most are in modest demand, and some are in absolutely zero demand. It is very difficult to tell which parts fall into that third group.

Another problem with parts is that they have to be disassembled, cleaned, cataloged, and sold. Most are inexpensive in comparison with the original gun, so it can take several sales to get the same amount of revenue.

Once you have the gun disassembled, you have one big chunk left over, this being the action or receiver—the controlled part of the gun. Sometimes there is a ready market for it, as in the case of certain military rifle actions, and that's where the law comes into play. But mainly, the action on parts guns will be a "throwaway" which, in addition to the record-keeping requirements, means you have to make your profit from the rest of the parts.

A final point for consideration is that, given the vast number of parts out there, there is a good chance that you will not have what any given buyer wants unless you maintain a large and varied inventory.

All of this assumes that you correctly identify and catalog the part or parts you have in hand. A relative of mine, who worked at the time as a designer for a large gun manufacturer, told me a story that puts this idea in perspective. When the company ended production of a certain model, it was customary to dispose of the parts on hand in two ways. Some were put on the shelf in anticipation of the company's need to cover warranty repairs on the guns already sold. The rest were sold in bulk to one of the parts houses, often a particular gigantic parts company in New York.

This company would come into the plant, catalog the parts, pack them up and move them to their own warehouse. Then, after the assembly line was dismantled, the parts people would sweep the floor under the line, gathering up all the mixed parts that had been dropped on the floor over the production life of the gun. These were put into a barrel marked "Floor Sweepings, XYZ Company, Model 123," there to remain until the company had the time and people to sort them all out.

Who knows what little treasures are sitting in a barrel in the back of that warehouse today? But the real surprise was what he related about the "regular parts" this company bought. As I said, they did their own cataloging. He watched one day as a barrel of pins was going out. The parts company man measured the pin's dimensions with a micrometer, wrote the description on a label, and pasted it to the outside of the barrel.

The label read, "Pin, 1.250x.0125" or something to that effect . . . no part number or cross reference to the model, because this pin might also be useable in other applications where the same size was called for.

My relative had designed the pin, and he realized that the parts man had measured it incorrectly, and so had labeled it incorrectly. When he called attention to this error, the labeler's response was, "Whatever . . . it's pretty close." These parts were, from that point on, basically lost to the world. No part made by that manufacturer carried those dimensions, and if the parts house selected on size, no order could ever be filled correctly from that barrel. And as my relative said, "They have tons and tons and tons of barrels just like that one in those warehouses."

On the flip side, there is a lot of good news about gun parts. First of all, the source material is always cheap. Parts guns sell for pennies on the dollar. Break the gun down into an average of 25-40 parts, and you have that many chances to make a profit. Realizing that demand will be varied for the various parts of a single gun, the objective is to make your profit quickly on the first few sales. If you have to sell out all of the parts to realize a full profit, you're pricing things way too low. There will be some parts, once sold, whose absence reflects on the value of the entire piece. I bought a "sporterized" Japanese Arisaka rifle for parting out recently, and the first customer wanted to buy just the screws that held the action to the trigger guard. Once these were sold, I had a bunch of Arisaka parts, rather than a sporterized Arisaka rifle.

Other than the action, gun parts usually are not regulated items, which means you can sell them as you please. Even eBay, which shuns guns, allows the sale of parts, which are generally small and can be mailed to buyers. Sales can be very profitable without being expensive, provided you buy right. But a couple of cautions are in order here.

Never represent the parts you are selling as being warranted by you. Always include a disclaimer that the buyer should have them checked by a competent gunsmith. The problem is that you have no control over what the buyer does with the part, so you will want to limit your liability.

Secondly, parts cost money and take up space. They take up that space even after you have recovered what you paid for the original parts gun. And, most importantly, you will probably have to decide whether you are going to be a gun trader or a parts dealer. There really aren't enough hours in a day to do both right.

As a parts guy, your days (and nights) will be spent in breaking down guns, cleaning the parts, cataloging the parts, handling correspondence and shipping. There are good profits to be made, if you are willing to learn your guns from the inside out . . . literally.

Another good portion of your day will be spent moving boxes of parts from one spot to another to find a particular box or part. I called a dealer once looking for a certain spring. He told me, "Yeah, I got some around here someplace. It'll cost you $2 for the spring, plus $20 for me to look for it." Obviously, we did no business that day, nor have we since. His attitude was indicative of what happens when you lose what I call "your fire," and that can be a problem in any line of work.

So let us suppose that a potential seller has called, and is bringing over a number of guns for your consideration. As they come out of their cases and bags, you realize from the first look that these are not prize pieces. A couple of them are inexpensive modern shotguns that are operational, though well used. Another one is a Civil War era piece that has been thoroughly sanded and reblued, along with one which is well patinaed. In fact it has so much patina that it is hard to work the action. Politely put, it is heavily rusted. Lastly, there are three .22 rifles, one with no sights, another with no forearm, and the third with no bolt.

For better or worse, you will encounter this scenario time and again. It has nothing to do with you or with your customer. Simply remember that you have to deal with the material that comes to you, so do it and move ahead quickly.

Of course, you could simply stop the whole process, tell the person his material simply doesn't have the condition you are looking for, and thank him for letting you look it over. This will undoubtedly invite the question, "Well, what would you offer for it?" If you refuse to make any offer at all, you may insult the person, so you might want to look a little more closely and see if there are some dollars winking at you from under the grime. If you do make an offer, be sure he understands that your offer is very low because you are buying the guns for parts, and not for resale as complete pieces.

You already know how to evaluate modern shotguns for resale using the TEK grid, and let us assume that they aren't making your clip level. The only other way to consider them would be as parts guns, even though they are operational.

The sanded and refinished Civil War piece will be off your radar screen as a resale item, and has little going for it except as a decorative wall hanger. You might be able to salvage the internals, but you probably won't be able to have it both ways. Sell it complete as a hanger (you will already have established a network of potential decorator buyers; if you don't have contacts ahead of time, the clock will already have begun ticking against your turn and profit targets), or scrap the externals and make your money from the parts.

Immediately upon giving notice to the world that you have parts for sale, you will begin to be hit with "yougottas," as in "you got a magazine (spring, lever, screw) for this?" Your conversations along these lines may give you an indication of the demand for certain parts. Keep good notes and use them to make a decision on this gun.

The rusty number also fails to meet your resale criteria. Its potential is similar to the refinished gun, but there's one thing going for it you'll want to check out. If it is complete, including reasonably sound wood, and simply needs an investment of time to get the rust off, you probably have a collector looking for it. Assume in your pricing that you aren't going to be doing the cleanup. On the other hand, if the gun isn't complete on the outside, it won't make it to the wall, so look at it for it's parts-only potential.

Finally, here comes that trio of .22s. The first is a bolt-action repeater in decent shape, except the front and rear sights are missing. Since sights don't just fall off, they were probably removed to make room for a scope, or for use on another gun. If you have a workable set of sights or a scope that you can install quickly, you may want to consider this one for resale, factoring in your costs for parts and labor. Otherwise, pass on it or plan to part it out.

The second little gem is a single shot from the early 1900s. It is sound, but the little wooden forearm and screw have parted company from the rest of the gun. How? Who knows, but they are gone. By the way, always, always ask the seller "do you by chance have any of the missing parts in a box someplace?" Usually the answer will be negative, but once in a while the question jogs a memory cell and the parts turn up.

If you have a market contact developed with a buyer who restores this sort of material, buy it right and move it quickly. Otherwise, part it out as a "group" . . . a batch of related parts sold in one lot. Tinkerers will pick up the whole batch just to get one part they need. They then part out the remainder, and so on down the line. In the meantime, you've made your money and moved on.

Unless you know precisely where to find a replacement forearm, don't even think about restoring the gun yourself. First of all, assume that the seller has already tried the usual channels, such as gun shows and parts houses. If you follow in his tracks, you'll find the same "out-of-stock," "had one a week ago" and "try again in 90 days" responses he did. Pass on the gun, or price it low and turn it quickly.

The third .22 is a single-shot bolt-action rifle in beautiful condition, with one exception . . . the bolt is missing. A bolt is actually an assembly made up of about 10 parts, any one of which can keep the gun in non-working status. To restore this one, you'll need to pull together all of the parts from perhaps several sources. It is unlikely that you'll be able to order the assembly in completed form, though sometimes they are available that way.

In either case, you'll be paying for each part separately . . . meaning $2 or $3 each for plain old coil springs. This sort of thing adds up quickly, and if you aren't in close touch with current parts prices, it's easy to get stung. And depending on the make and model of the gun, the parts may simply not be available at any price.

So what about simply parting out what we have . . . a bolt-less single shot? Take away the bolt on a gun like this and there is very little left beside the barrel, stock and trigger. Hard to make any money here. Pass on it or get the seller to throw it into the deal for a couple of dollars . . . literally a couple of dollars. Mark it up to $10, and push it to someone willing to search for a bolt. Meanwhile, your money goes back to work.

Gun traders also run into "boxes" of parts. You'll find these on tables at gun shows, flea markets and similar venues. If your objective is simply to increase your parts inventory, this is a good way to do it. If you'd rather make money, though, this approach should be way down on your list.

I was at a show recently and met a dealer whose specialty was small revolvers in the "just-barely antiques" category and early percussion guns. Along the way, he'd acquired many damaged and incomplete guns. Rather than taking the trouble to dismantle them and keep the parts together, he had put all the hammers in one box, the triggers in another, etc. All were unmarked, of course. "Need a hammer for that H&R pocket pistol? Dig through the box there and see what you find. Cost you a dollar if you find what you want." I watched a customer work for an hour matching up his broken hammer against specimens in the box, and though he came close several times, ultimately, there was no cigar. My feeling is that the dealer simply couldn't decide to commit to getting into the parts game and wasn't willing to do the cataloging. As a result, he had the worst of both worlds; he lugged the stuff around and saw few sales.

You'll also run into boxes of parts from estates at flea markets and yard sales. Always look these over carefully. Much of the contents will be worth little or nothing, but sometimes you'll find some real goodies.

26. ACCESSORIES

Some guns come from the factory equipped with certain accessories, such as sights or slings. Whenever these are absent from the gun, the price goes down. When they are encountered stand-alone, especially those associated with older guns, they are often in heavy demand from people who want to "complete" their own gun.

Beyond accessories originally included with specific models, there are three basic kinds of shooting accessories to consider as a gun trader, because you'll often find them included as part of the packages offered to you.

SCOPES AND SIGHTS

The most common accessories are sights and scopes. Sights will only have an impact on the package when they are compatible with the gun, but were not factory original.

You'll see this with target guns in particular. In fact, many times the guns were priced from the dealer without sights, giving the buyer the option of adding those of his own choosing. Quite often, the sight sets cost as much as the rifle, and these competition iron sights have developed into an active market of their own. If you are going to play in that sandbox, do your homework just as thoroughly as you did for the gun itself.

One step down from these Olympic-grade sights is the top-end group of metallic sights that, prior to the common use of scopes, were the best sighting option available to shooters. Although you don't see them offered as original equipment today, collectors still pay good money for them as add-ons and upgrades to pieces in their collections.

At the bottom of the ladder are the relatively inexpensive metallic sights, of the Williams economy type. These are quality sights and they do their job well, but there just isn't an active sub-market for them. The guidance here is as before . . . stay in your niche and study the subject before you move in.

Telescopic sights are a little tougher nut to crack. The scopes you find will fall into two groups, the first, in grades from top to bottom, being those from currently active companies. Production scopes aren't particularly collectible. Models come and go according to the whims of the marketing department.

Those at the bottom end of the quality pyramid still work pretty well for most shooters under most conditions. Most are semi-disposable . . . cheap enough so that if one fails, another can go on in its place. You'll find these scopes on .22s and many "deer rifles," and they add little to the price of the gun.

Next in line are the majority of scopes, giving good optics and excellent resistance to the weather, for a moderate price. This is about as far up the quality line as most shooters go, because these scopes will do the job. The difficulty for the gun trader is that the seller sees the gun and scope together as a package, while the trader understands that most scopes lose value as soon as they are installed.

As an example, consider a scope with a suggested retail of $750. You'll probably see it retailing regularly for someplace around $550 to $600, and you'll see it in excellent condition at shows, by itself, for $300 to $350. The owner looks at his scope and sees $750 in value, while you know you have to buy it at about $200 to make it work out. That's a big gap to bridge. If at all possible, price the scope and the gun separately when you make your offer. Anticipate that the seller may want to keep the scope, and base your offer on the gun accordingly.

At the top end of this group are the high-magnification, super-spec scopes intended for target and long-range varmint work. They will usually be found on guns of similar high quality, and the total package price can easily be double the value of the gun by itself. Always treat this grade of scope as an entity unto itself, almost as though you are purchasing two guns. Figure your offer and selling prices from the angle of selling the two separately, knowing the scope will always be the tougher sell.

The second major category in sights and scopes includes the high-end old timers . . . the Feckers, the Hensoldts, etc. These were absolutely state-of-the-art products in their day, and are now very collectible. When you see them offered for sale by themselves, buy or pass as your expertise dictates.

Finding them installed on the gun you are considering is a different matter. When the scope simply belongs on the gun, treat the whole thing as a package and price it accordingly. This will usually be a gun from the 1920s to the early 1950s, perhaps a custom-built varmint or target gun, and the price for the package will probably be higher than the total of the two pieces sold separately. If you know what you are looking at, and know the market for it, fine. If not, pass on the purchase.

HOLSTERS

When you buy a handgun, it is quite common for the owner to have accessories available for it, most generally at least a holster.

Holsters come in two flavors. The first is the "I carried it in this" category, where the leather is simply one of a number of brands made for use with that particular model of handgun—a commercial product, much like a sling or gun case. From the gun trader's perspective, such a holster adds virtually no value to the deal at all. If the seller wants to toss it in, okay. You can then toss it into the "stuff" box at home, waiting until you do a gun show where you can offer it for $1, or run a bunch of them together on eBay and hope for $10 for the lot. Sometimes you can seal a deal by telling the seller, "You keep the extras and I'll take just the gun for this much money."

The other flavor involves leather that would always have been associated with the gun, as in the case of a military holster. Holsters properly marked and in good condition can be prized by collectors, and can add a good chunk of money to the price of the gun. They come in a number of varieties, usually with markings indicating the maker and perhaps the unit to which the gun was issued. Serious students in this area will frequently buy a holster even though they have no gun to go with it, recognizing it to be an uncommon and desirable item.

A collector told me he sometimes used the ownership of the holster as a justification for going out and buying the gun. This logic, perfectly acceptable to collectors, may be less well received by spouses.

One place you might find this sort of "gun-with-holster" package is in the case of trophies brought home by solders, especially those who served in Europe during WWII. Unfortunately, by the time the gun and holster finished their wanderings, the holster may not be the one originally issued. The gun fits into it, but not well. The seller will assert "that's exactly the way Uncle Moe brought it home," and that's probably true, but the match up is still incorrect. Don't pay any sort of premium unless the holster has value in its own right.

A related scenario involves holsters and saddle scabbards associated with antique arms. By themselves, unless ownership by a historical figure can be authenticated, these accessories have little value unless they are in pristine condition. But a Winchester carbine found in a worn saddle scabbard, or a Colt Peacemaker in its belted holster, immediately commands more attention.

It isn't so much that the price goes up, though it does, but rather that the salability of the gun skyrockets. This is especially true with "Western" or "Cowboy" guns, or with Civil War items. Don't ever separate the two components, and be very careful to maintain the condition of the accessory. Sometimes that means leaving it alone. It survived this long without your ministrations, so be gentle with it.

I saw an example of this "association" phenomenon at a show I did some years ago. I had acquired a Remington percussion revolver on the previous evening. It was not a ruster, but it was badly in need of a cleanup, which I had intended to do before offering it for sale.

The revolver came to me with a "border" style holster, one that had obviously been with the gun for a long time, if not from the beginning. It was not a handsome piece of leather, and not in fine condition, but it just screamed "Authentic!" when you saw it

As I was unpacking my wares for display at the show, dealers descended on me like vultures on the plains of Africa. I told each one that I planned to clean up the gun before selling it, but one guy in particular kept coming back, asking "what do you want for it now, as is?"

I was tired and getting a little irritated, so I finally threw out a price about three times greater than I had planned to ask for when the gun was ready for sale. He calmly reached into his pocket, counted out the cash, and said "I just love to find them like this when they haven't been messed with." I admit, even today, that I would like to have given the gun the TLC it needed, just to see what it looked like, but my job as a gun trader was to make the money and move on . . . so I did.

One other class of accessory that you will see being hawked at shows and in papers like Shotgun News is military surplus. If you are interested in militaria, go for it, but it really isn't a part of gun trading. Ammo cans, tripods, bandoleers, etc., unlike scopes and magazines, aren't going to help the sale of the gun at all, and will soak up your time and money.

27. SALES TAX (AND YOUR SALES TAX NUMBER)

If you are questionably blessed, as most of us are, by living where your gun trading will be subject to sales-tax rules, register with your state agency as a sales-tax collector, get a sales-tax number and collect the tax. In most places, private sales are exempt from collecting these fees, but businesses aren't. Sure, it's a nuisance, but "rules is rules," and if you fail to collect the tax, you may be held personally liable for it. So take the easy road on this one and start off right.

You may find that your tax number will save you from having to pay sales tax on some purchases, but this is usually the case only when you are buying for resale. Buying for use (as in buying cleaning patches), whether for personal or business purposes, doesn't meet that criteria.

28. INSURANCE

The guns that you own, as a private individual, are probably covered under your home owner's or renter's insurance policy. I say probably because different insurers do things differently, and some require that specific items, such as guns, jewelry and special collections, be covered either partly or completely by a rider.

As a gun trader, however, it is important for you to understand that your sales inventory is most likely not covered by that same insurance, and you should contact your agent to be sure. Most likely, you will need to have a separate commercial policy to cover the business's guns. Your agent may be able to supply that coverage, but don't be surprised if he can't. Many carriers have dropped firearms as "risky." If you have a problem finding the coverage, or with the rates, get in touch with the NRA or NSSF. They can direct you to several companies who specialize in insuring the gun trade.

Insurance companies issue coverage for different types of risk—for both the premises and your inventory against fire and other perils, as well as liability coverage if someone is injured on your premises, injured with a product you sold them, and so on. So you may need several types of insurance, depending on what services you offer.

If you are simply selling new guns (not the recommended spot on the CDS table, but anyway . . .), you may be able to get away with simple business coverage and standard liability, the same as any other type of seller would obtain. If you deal in used guns, or do repairs on them, you may want to get product liability insurance. In today's legal environment, injured parties sue everyone and everything in sight. They bet that the cost of defending the suit will lead to a settlement, even in cases without real merit. Selling your inventory with the disclaimer that it "should be inspected by a competent gunsmith before use" sounds good, but it probably doesn't provide much protection.

29. SECURITY

Although one of our major focus items with the TEK system is rapid turnover, you will usually have inventory on hand. The number of guns, and the associated value, will go up and down over time, but it is prudent to take steps to safeguard whatever inventory you do have. The more you advertise, and the more you have people at your place of business, the more likely it is that a bad guy will learn of your situation and consider trying to separate you from your assets.

Our objective is to "harden" your environment so as to make the next person's assets look more attractive to this bad guy and his friends. We want to motivate him to leave us alone, and the most effective way to do that is to make him realize that he will get nabbed before he can get away with the goods. So we do two things: alert the authorities of this criminal activity, and then keep the baddie from getting at the inventory until help arrives.

In some areas, alarms and safe-type protection are required by insurance companies and also by local law. Alarm systems using current technology are quite good at telling the difference between an intruder and a stray mouse—a very important distinction, because false alarms will dull your response to the real thing.

Choose sensors, cameras, and systems that will alert you before entry is achieved. Use a central-station service to contact the police directly as soon as the alarm comes in. Most of these systems use phone lines to call the monitoring agency, so be sure that your lines are armored, or that your audible alarm will trigger if the lines are cut.

Another technique, though more costly, uses radio to contact the agencies. Candidly evaluate you needs and select your protection accordingly. The more value you are protecting, the more likely you are to attract skilled crooks. You probably couldn't keep them out indefinitely, but if you delay them until the cops get there, you win.

So assume that the door, window, whatever has been breached. The local alarm is screaming, the appropriate agency has been notified, and the sheriff is on his way. We need to keep the crook at bay for about 10 or 15 minutes at most. The most effective way to do this is with a series of locked doors and a safe. If you have a separate room for your business, you may want to harden the whole room, effectively making it a giant safe. Metal doors and multiple strong locks will create the delay you need. Even a closet can be used with this method. Some line the interior walls with thin steel plates.

If you don't have a spare room, or think that might be a bit "much," plan on using protective metal cabinets or a safe. The cabinets will certainly add some of the delay time you need, and that can be increased by adding strong hasp-type locks. Be sure the cabinet is secured to the wall and/or floor. A major point in favor of the cabinet is cost. You can buy several cabinets for the price of one medium-size safe.

Many people who decide they want a safe are unsure about which one to buy.

Regardless of the brand, safes come in either "plain" or "fire" versions. A plain safe is just that. It has thick metal walls, a strong door and a heavy-duty combination lock. The door is normally secured by bars or bolts that cam into the safe body when the handle is rotated. To open the safe, these bolts must be withdrawn into the door itself. If the handle is smashed or torn off, the linkage from the handle to the bolts is destroyed and the bolts must then be defeated individually by the bad guy . . . very time consuming.

Fastening the safe to the floor or wall adds delay and keeps someone from simply dragging it away to a more private place. Using a safe equipped with wheels or casters, of course, works in just the opposite way.

Fire safes have the same features as the plain variety, but add a layer of insulation between the walls. This also increases the weight of the unit. No matter what the salesman implies, there is no such thing as a fire-proof safe. The insulation serves to delay an increase in temperature inside when heat is applied outside. The thicker the insulation, the slower the interior temperature rises.

When you look at a fire safe, it will have a fire rating. If, for example, the rating is 250 degrees/one hour, it means that the level of insulation will limit the temperature increase to no more than 250 degrees when the exterior is subjected to a temperature of 1,500 degrees for an hour. Assuming a beginning temperature of, say, 80 degrees, the total temperature inside would be 330 degrees after an hour. This is still below the combustion point of paper (451 F), so things inside are getting hot, but not burning.

Realize, however, that if the outside of the safe is exposed to 1,500 degrees for an hour, you probably have a whole different set of problems to deal with, not the least of which is that the "upstairs safe" may now be the "downstairs safe"! Sometimes, when you look at the edge of the door on a fire safe, you will see what appears to be exposed insulation, and the thought may occur that this is shoddy construction. The material you see is a fusible lining at the door edges. When subjected to about 200 degrees, this material expands, creating an airtight seal to keep outside hot air outside.

Prices for safes vary based on three factors other than brand. The first is the exterior appearance. The less expensive finish is the powder coat; the gloss finish costs more. You can get works of art added to the outside, gold-plated handles, humidity-control systems, adjustable racks and shelving, and built-in lights and alarms. Many of these features are intended for buyers who want to make their safes an acceptable piece of furniture in the house. If that is your situation, and you have to "sell" the idea to someone, these features are a good talking point.

A better point, though, is the idea that the safe can be used to protect things besides guns: cameras, jewelry, collections, papers, photographs, etc. Placing the papers and photos in a small firebox effectively increases the fire protection level. If you have to keep the safe in a place where it may be subject to high humidity, consider installing a low heat source, such as a light build or "dry-rod" to keep things dry.

Prices also increase as the level of protection rises. Added resistance to theft comes from thicker bolts, a larger number of bolts, heavier-gauge metal walls, "breakaway" handles, interior hinges (exposed hinges can be cut off) and lockable combination dials.

The last price kicker is the size. Capacity costs money, but one 20-gun safe will cost less than two 10-gun safes. On the other hand, a big advantage of two smaller safes is that even if one is broken into, only half the inventory is threatened. As you decide on what size to purchase, consider where you will keep it, and whether the floor will support it without reinforcement. Also think (in advance) about how you will get the safe from where it is to where you want it to be. Some "light haulers" will get the safe to your front door, but balk at going up or down stairs. And are there any sharp turns to negotiate? Plan ahead.

The most useful rule of thumb I can give you is to buy a safe at least twice as large as you think you need. That sounds extreme, but it invariably happens that you will find more things that need a "safe place" than you can imagine. Select an interior partition system that meets your expected needs. Long guns need vertical storage, even if in rows several deep. Handguns and other small items can utilize adjustable shelving most efficiently.

Finally, remember that alarms, safes and cabinets can provide protection only if they are used. Alarm systems that are not armed provide only visual deterrence. Cabinets that are not locked serve to keep dust off the inventory, but that's about all. Safes are the biggest offenders, though. Folks love to close the door and turn the handle, but many times they don't spin the dial. Of course it takes longer to open it again if you spin the dial, but that's the idea, right? And when you buy a key-lockable combination dial, spin the dial before you lock the key lock. That way, the crook has to crack two locks instead of one.

30. ENVIRONMENTAL PROTECTION

The biggest enemy of your inventory is humidity, and the next biggest is your own 10 fingers (and those of your customers). Humidity control is an issue in most locations at least in the summertime, but in some places, you need to be careful all year long. Cabinets and safes should be equipped with a drying device, such as a small light bulb. If at all possible, also use a room dehumidifier during those seasons when your heating system is not running. These steps will reduce the opportunity for moisture to collect and cause rusting. It's far easier to prevent the rust than to remove it.

Now, about those mitts of yours: The skin on everyone's fingers carries some amount of acid, and that acid can etch a fingerprint right into a metal surface. Most people don't have an extremely acid touch, but enough do that you have to protect against it. Several remedies are possible, such as using a rust preventative on modern guns that carry no patina. But the best method is to use light white-cotton gloves when handling the most delicate pieces. Be sure they fit snugly so that you don't complicate a rust problem with a dropping problem, and keep a spare set on hand for your customer to use, too.

The next few finer points cover how you can be your own best customer—the trader-collector. Hanging on the wall in my shop is a long list of guns I've sold and wish I still had. What made them unusual was the fact that these were fairly common guns, but ones rarely found in good shape . . . and my specimens were in mint condition. So why did I sell them? I sold them to keep the stake turning and growing. Mind you, I don't regret selling them. I just wish I still had them. As I did, you'll find that unless you are over-endowed with funds, you simply cannot mix collecting and trading in the same stake. If you try to, you will soon see your stake hanging on the wall rather than working in an ad or on the web.

Some people will switch from collector to trader, and back again, as they reach their collection goals. They have limited funds available, so they need to liquidate the existing collection in order to move on to the next. These folks are collectors at heart, sort of. I say sort of because a true collector seeks perfection in every component in the group, often going many months between acquisitions. Trader-collectors are more interested in the acquisition of pieces, not necessarily in building a perfect collection. I say all of this meaning absolutely no disrespect for trader-collectors. They're having fun and that's what matters to them. Maybe they make a little, maybe they lose a little, but they had fun without having to follow the rigid discipline of the true gun trader . . . and they also didn't make the kind of money a true gun trader can make.

All of this notwithstanding, if you simply cannot part with some of your gun trading acquisitions, put some guidelines in place for yourself.

First, mentally set yourself up as a customer for your gun trading efforts. Take the same approach to guns that will potentially wind up in your own cabinet as you would to your regular gun trading stock. If you would normally pay $500 for a gun, don't pay $600 just because you want it for your collection. If you do buy it, and would normally sell it for $650, move $650 from your collection fund to your gun trading fund . . . not mentally, but physically. Never mix the two funds together, and never "owe" the gun trading fund. Keep that money separate, distinct and working.

Finally, be careful to avoid focusing on your looking at only guns that have a collector interest for you, if that focus comes at the expense of passing up better gun trading opportunities.

31. KEEPING RECORDS

The need to keep good records stems from two sources. First of all, if you hold an FFL, you are required to maintain certain information regarding the acquisition and disposition of your inventory. Secondly, your friends at the IRS will want to know how much extra money was in that pocket when you turned it inside out, so records must be maintained on the income and expenses of the business.

Financial data that you will need for tax purposes include two basic breakdowns—what came in and what went out. The difference is, or should be, what you have left. That's what the tax man wants to talk about. In the absence of your data to the contrary, he'll assume that you had no expenses at all, and so will treat all of "what came in" as "what's left."

The simplest bookkeeping test is a very common sense one: What's the total amount of revenue; what's the total of expenses? You should have funds in the cash box equal to the difference. Whenever you suspect your records aren't giving an accurate picture, apply this test to be sure that the numbers are correct, at least in the aggregate.

Revenue includes every penny that comes to you from a customer. Some revenue will go to you and some, like sales tax, may go to the government. Be sure that you don't include sales tax as part of your income calculation. The money belongs to the government . . . you're just the temporary custodian.

Expense includes every penny you pay out to someone in furtherance of your business, along with "costs" you incur that don't actually come out of your pocket, such as depreciation (wear and tear). Careful tracking of small expenses will make a big difference to your bottom line. Remember that you can do well with each individual trade, but if the other expenses you incur are out of line, all that profit can go right down the tubes.

Expenses such as rent, advertising, payroll, security systems, etc., are not directly attributable to any specific gun, so they are deducted after the gross profit is figured. (In Chapter 1, I said, "We're interested only in net profit," but we have to calculate gross profit first, then deduct expenses, to arrive at "net" . . . the profit that matters). Be sure you identify money paid for auction fees, mileage, postage, office supplies, packaging materials, cleaning supplies, insurance, telephone, subscriptions, and all the other little things. They add up in a hurry.

You'll maintain some records because you are required to. But the most important data you keep because you want to know what it can tell you. When you use the TEK system, you have to tally the score and then use that score to adjust the way you use TEK.

In addition to any other data you keep, track the financial and turn performance on every single gun you buy and sell using TEK. Use paper if you need to, or a computer if you have one. The layout and column headings aren't important; the data is what matters. Track the following:

1. Make and model (for comparison when you encounter another one of these)
2. Source (perhaps you can go back to this source for more material)
3. Date of purchase (day, month and year)
4. Planned cost (TEK offer price plus planned extras, such as repairs)
5. Amount paid to the seller (cash plus your asking price of any traded item)
6. Amount of other expense incurred (shipping, tax, repairs, etc.)
7. Planned selling price (TEK selling price)
8. Planned turn target (TEK turn goal)
9. Actual date of sale (day, month, year)

10. Actual turn realized (number of months between purchase and sale, divided by 12)
11. Sale price (without tax)
12. Sales expenses (shipping, auction site fees, etc)
13. Profit (sale price less selling expense, less cost of gun, less other expenses; see example)
14. Profit Margin (profit as a percentage of sale price)
15. Annualized rate of return (profit margin adjusted to an annual rate)

Now that you have this long list of data, what can you learn from it? For each gun, compare the planned profit to the actual profit. How did you do? If you make less than you planned, figure out why. Did you decide that the market-price estimate wasn't realistic? Did a customer promise and then bail out? Try to pinpoint just what happened.

If the sale price exceeded the estimate, we need to understand what happened there, too. This may seem unimportant, because more profit is always better, but the point is that we did something we hadn't planned to do, and that isn't "better." Did you run into a customer who made an opening offer higher than our planned selling price? Did you find that an anticipated repair wasn't required after all? Again, we need to understand what caused us to miss the target.

I was spotting for a buddy doing some long-range target shooting one day, and we had two large targets set up at 500 yards. After some warm-ups, he steadied on the bull and squeezed off a shot. That bullet landed about as close to the exact center of the target as one could imagine. I looked at it through the spotting scope for a moment and then began congratulating him on his fine shot.

He leaned over, checked through the spotter himself, and then lifted his head slowly. I could see a glum expression on his face, and couldn't understand it. Most people would go a lifetime and not make that shot. He explained, "I was aiming at the other target."

What matters to us is achieving not just good results, but the planned results. Did we meet our anticipated turn speed? When you figure the "time of possession," do so in "days," then convert that answer to 30-day "months." If you had the gun for 60 days, that equates to two months, or a turn of six. Similarly, 45 days would be one-and-a-half months, etc. One of the real motivators in this game is the annualized return on a gun turned over in one week.

Here again, if we went long, we need to understand why. Delays in getting an auction started, repairs taking longer than expected, a local show being cancelled, a buyer backing out . . . all things that can happen. We need to decide whether what happened "this time" was a one-shot deal, or whether we need to adjust our thinking to anticipate more frequent occurrences of the same thing. The same is true if we turned the gun faster than anticipated. If we do that on a regular basis, perhaps we should be raising our sights a little and factoring a better turn rate into our TEK profile.

One sale, or even two or three, probably won't give us enough of a trend to adjust our strategy, but by the time we've had, say, six or eight sales in hand, we can probably start to see a pattern.

Look at both the average and the range. The problem with averages, used by themselves, is that if your right hand is frozen and your left hand is on fire, on average, you're comfortable. So if you missed half your turns high, and the other half low, on average you were correct all of the time. In reality, we need to see these actuals coming in very close to plan, whether high or low. That's far more important than being accurate "on average."

If you see that your profit margin is "on plan," but you are consistently low on the turns, you'll need to make one of two adjustments. Either go back to the TEK system and, accepting the turns you are seeing as the norm, select another margin target, or find a more creative way to move sales through faster.

If you are missing the planned profit margin, but hitting the turns correctly, it could mean that you are "bailing out" too quickly . . . accepting the first offer that is made, even if it is below your plan. Generally, the window of opportunity on turns has about 30 days to it, so the only time to consider accepting a low offer would be either when you are close to the end of the window, or when you are convinced that this offer is the best you can get. In the latter case, if you think this is as good as you can do, close the deal promptly. This will at least salvage what you can on the turns side.

The other possible cause for missing the profit point is failing to include an allowance in the offer price for repairs, parts, etc. Of course, if you find some sort of hidden damage that could only be detected by a total disassembly, well, at least learn from the experience and try to be more discerning next time. But if this becomes a repeated pattern, you'll need to change either your examination pattern or else do a lot more studying.

Missing problems is most likely to happen when you are working out at the edges of your knowledge niche. If you find that repairs are taking longer than planned because you are doing them yourself and you run out of time each day, you'll need to either eliminate this level of repair from your consideration, or factor into the offer the cost of having it done professionally. If your professional is missing his time commitments to you, find another professional.

32. TRANSFERS

As a gun trader, your principal business activity will always be the buying and selling of firearms. Along the way, however, you may discover a market for some other services directly related to gun trading. The most common of these services are transfers, appraisals and consignment sales. A transfer may go something like this:

Joe called you a couple of weeks ago looking for a Winchester Model 54 rifle. You didn't have one on hand and didn't expect to have one coming in right away. Today, Joe called again and said that he has found one in East Clabber, Oklahoma. A collector there has one he is willing to sell, but the man said Joe would have to find a "transfer agent." Joe wants you to handle the transfer.

I mentioned this scenario a couple of times in earlier chapters, but what is actually involved in providing this service? Think of it as the buyer "renting" your FFL for a fee. You would send a signed copy of your FFL to the seller, who will then ship the gun to you for transfer to the buyer. You record the gun into and out of your FFL bound book, and insure that the form 4473 and background check are properly completed. This is straightforward enough, but how much should you charge?

Transfers aren't part of gun trading. They are an opportunity to pick up some additional income while moving along, simultaneously, with your mainstream gun trading activity. For that reason, the TEK tables don't apply.

Transfers come in two versions. The first is a plain transfer. The buyer handles all of the correspondence, arranges for the sale, and takes care of all financial matters. You just have to send the FFL copy to the dealer, receive the gun and pass it along. For the service, most dealers charge between $25 and $50 per gun, with a volume discount for multiple guns received at the same time. If this service is subject to sales tax in your area, your customer would be responsible to you for only the tax on your service. If the purchase itself is taxable, that is for the seller and buyer to work out between themselves.

You may also find that the customer wants you to ship a gun out for him. Sometimes this is because of the carrier regulations, but mostly it is because the customer isn't comfortable with packing the gun properly and getting it safely and securely shipped. Charge your regular transfer fee, and then extra for the packing, the packaging materials, and transportation to the shipping point.

The second form of transfer is the "buy it for me" situation: A customer has located the gun he wants, but would like you to handle getting the funds to the seller. If the buyer gives you the money for the purchase up front, you'd probably only charge him for the transfer plus a bit extra for getting the money order.

On the other hand, if he asks you to put up your own funds, agreeing to pay you when he picks up the gun, you are entitled to a full margin on the transaction because the risk is all yours. Also, money tied up in this sort of transaction cannot be working in the TEK system at the same time. The customer needs to understand this beforehand.

In both of these "buy it for me" transactions, you are responsible for collecting any applicable sales tax on the deal and on your transfer service. All of which can be a motivator for that customer to use your transfer service exclusively. And that gives you some added income without heavily distracting from your gun trading.

33. CONSIGNMENTS

When an individual sells something "on consignment," it means that the person doing the actual selling, the dealer, is not the owner of the property. It has been "consigned" to him, and title remains with the owner until the sale has been completed. The seller is simply the custodian, which means that the owner can take the item back when he wishes, unless some other agreement has been made.

Because the seller does not have his own funds tied up in the item he is selling, he is entitled to a smaller return on the sale than might otherwise be the case. Many owners understand that they can net more money by selling to the end user on a consignment basis than they would make by selling to a reseller.

I know a number of dealers who simply will not get involved in consignment sales. They will offer to buy the gun from the owner, but if that doesn't work, they walk away. Why? I don't know for sure, unless it is that they have so many guns to look at, they have no time available. Most dealers who handle consignments do so for a percentage of the selling price. This insures that the interests of the owner and the seller are in synch. The higher the selling price, the more each of them makes.

Consignments, like transfers, are not a part of mainline gun trading activity. Of course, when any consignment is offered, your first look at it should be with purchase in mind, according to your TEK recommendation. Since you make no guarantee on how quickly a consignment might be sold, the owner may decide to take your offer right away, just to get things settled. Since the consignment deal is already on the table, he will understand that his net profit will be higher than if he sells to you, and that unless/until the gun is sold, he gets nothing. "A bird in the hand," etc.

He will undoubtedly want to know how much you believe the gun will sell for. Because he has already turned down your best offer for an outright purchase, giving him your assessment of the market value does no harm at all. He will compare your purchase offer to his potential net from the consignment, and sometimes, if the gap is not too great, he may reconsider selling directly to you.

When you take on a consignment, you are obligated to act in the seller's best interest, which will almost always also be in your best interest. If the piece should be cleaned or repaired to be salable, tell the owner that. Whenever service or repair is needed, recommend it only if the net to the customer, after payment of the repair fee, will not be reduced. If the problem is serious, and he doesn't want to correct it, don't handle the sale. And turn down the sale if the item is outside of your knowledge niche, or if the condition is such that it would have a negative impact on your regular sales. Some dealers will accept only those consignments that do not compete with their own stock. Be sure to lay out with the owner how such a conflict will be handled, for instance, when you have in inventory a gun the same as the one he wishes to sell. Which of them will you push?

Fees for consignments are usually based on a sliding scale, with the percentage decreasing as the selling price goes up. The fee should never be flat for all sales, however, because your risk, as custodian, increases as the value of the gun goes up. Should something happen to it while in your possession, you owe the owner the same amount as if it had been sold. Consignments will take up more of your time than will transfers, so charge enough to make it worthwhile. Most dealers charge from 10 percent on the high-end guns to 30 percent for the least expensive pieces.

34. APPRAISALS

When you write a gun appraisal, you are purely selling your expertise. Most customers seeking an appraisal are doing so for insurance or estate purposes. Sometimes you'll also be asked for valuations by couples untying the matrimonial knot—which means sometimes the request comes from the owner, and sometimes it comes from a lawyer or insurance agent (who may have other clients with similar needs). In any case, these customers are asking for your advice as an expert, and are willing to pay for it.

Think of appraisals as pre-buying work. In other words, these guns may or may not be put up for sale immediately after being appraised, but it is likely that they will come onto the market eventually. And guess who will likely get the first opportunity to buy them . . .

An appraisal is a written opinion based on experience. It isn't a legal document, but it should certainly be written as a professional document, with proper grammar, correct spelling and punctuation, and a crisp presentation. It this isn't your strength, get hold of a well-written appraisal and follow the same approach. Some appraisers create a basic format for each type of firearm (rifle, shotgun, revolver, and pistol) and then just fill in the blanks. The technique works, but it isn't as effective as a smoothly written evaluation.

Generally, it is a bad idea to write an appraisal of any gun you don't have right in front of you. But suppose the customer doesn't want to leave the gun with you? My solution is to use a note-taking form, which is essentially a mental jogger list of things to look at. Even with this, though, you may still miss checking something that is relevant to the value. Should this happen, your only recourse is to go back and look at the gun again. You might also take some photos, but that adds to the time and should also add to the fee.

Appraisals should be based on NRA grading standards, and values should be given at the current regional retail market level. If there is a particular fact of supply, demand or regulation affecting the value, make note of that.

I recall writing an appraisal for a decrepit muzzle-loading pistol that appeared to have been cobbled together someplace in the Middle East. For reasons known only to the person who did it, the stock had been heavily and quite inartistically inlaid with thick gold sheet material. At the time, gold was selling for over $800 an ounce, so the appraisal indicated that the basic gun was worth around $30, but the gold inlays brought the current value up to about $5,000. When the gold market plunged shortly thereafter, so did the appraised value of the gun.

Write the appraisal in the same way that you inspect the gun. Start at one end and go to the other. Describe what you see and what it implies. If you cannot identify the maker, try to make at least an attribution, or price it by what similar guns are selling for. If repairs or other service would have a positive impact on the evaluation, include that information. And always, when you render a value verdict, be sure to include mention that this is a retail value, and the seller should not expect to receive this amount from a dealer. In this way, your retail evaluation will not come back to haunt you later, should you have an opportunity to make an offer on the gun.

Appraisal writing is a good way to expand your niche knowledge. You'll find that if you weren't familiar with a particular make or model before you wrote the appraisal, you certainly will be afterward. This makes it an activity that contributes directly to your success as a gun trader. ■

NOTES

TAKING IT
TO THE
NEXT LEVEL...

ADVANCED
GUN TRADING

After you have been gun trading for awhile and have a pretty fair knowledge of the guns and the market, you may feel confident enough to move into the advanced aspects of the game. You'll be dealing with more expensive guns, and working some of the finer points of demand. But you will still be figuring your offers from the TEK-I table. Eventually, however, you may have to move to the TEK-II level. This step should not be taken lightly, but it is the inevitable destination for the successful gun trader.

I say inevitable because up to now, we've been concentrating on making sure that our pipeline stays full, that we select carefully from that pipeline, and that we buy right from that selection. These things will become almost automatic for the experienced gun trader, but then a different problem will almost certainly arise. It will become more and more difficult to find enough sellers willing to accept our offers to buy. This is because the TEK-I table used up to now is geared to making a better-than-average return on each transaction, and by virtue of turn power, turning that transaction return into an outstanding annual one. That provides the novice and intermediate gun trader with some protections against making a serious error. Even if you make a modest mistake, the margins prevent it from becoming a major problem.

But those protective margins can increasingly become a hindrance as your volume levels climb higher and higher. In more and more of your transactions, you'll find yourself hitting the limit of the TEK-recommended buy price without getting the seller to go along. Don't get discouraged when and if you reach this point, though. By taking advantage of your expertise, and by making some adjustments to the TEK numbers, we can still move right ahead.

By the same token, though, don't move to TEK-II unless or until you have to. If you can keep your stake invested fully with TEK-I level offers, you will be ahead of the game. TEK-II is intended for use only when your local competition and/or your stake size push you out of TEK-I.

35. TEK-I VS. TEK-II

When you look at the TEK-II table, you'll see that it differs from TEK-I only in that the band of potential margins is much narrower, and the turn options are tighter. The transaction margins are smaller and the turn targets are increased. All of this is necessary because, rather than looking for high returns on each transaction, we will be looking completely at "annualized returns."

We can define an annualized return as the actual return on the sale adjusted to the equivalent return on a 12-month basis. In other words, if we make one percent in one month, that's equivalent to 12 percent in one year. Note: The underlying assumption with annualizing a rate is that you can do it during each time period during the year. Saying that one percent a month is equal to 12 percent a year is only true if you make that return each month! If you only make it once, then put the money under the mattress, your annual return is one percent . . . period.

Any activity that promises high returns is bound to attract participants, and gun trading is no exception. Using TEK-I, we might seek a 20 percent return in three months. Annualized, that's a 120 percent return, which is pretty fantastic. Can it be done? Sure it can, and as an experienced gun trader, you've done it many times. But you're trying to do it time after time after time, and so is every other experienced gun trader. And so the thinking quickly becomes, "I have a customer all lined up for this gun, so I can shave a percentage point or two off my TEK return and still come out way ahead. It won't be 20 percent, but I can live on 18 percent . . . or 15 percent . . . or five percent . . . or three percent." The key idea here is that "I have a customer all lined up for this gun," not "I can live on only three percent." It is precisely because I have a customer all lined up, or know exactly where I can find an immediate buyer, that I can work on an annualized basis.

Once you have a fair amount of gun trading experience under your belt, you'll find yourself making extremely rapid evaluations of the condition of the guns you encounter. The width and depth of your knowledge niche will allow you to decide quickly on the relative scarcity of the piece and the customer demand for it. You'll have a quick reference on hand for your customer's "wants." All that's left at that point will be to decide on the market value of the gun so you can make an offer using the TEK-II table. You are much more apt to make the deal using this table, but remember that you are also dropping much of the "safety net" built into the TEK-I table.

Once again, be careful about jumping into the use of the TEK-II tables, and do so only if you have to. They are built around certain assumptions that have to happen if you are to be successful. The key assumptions are that you can keep your stake fully invested and that you are turning your stock very rapidly. If you miss on either of these points, your profit will suffer.

Let's assume that you are having trouble keeping your stake invested. Does that mean you should automatically move to TEK-II? It may, but only if you can't correct the problem within TEK-I. If you are a full-time gun trader, you should be looking at a minimum of at least 50 guns a week, not counting gun shows, and at least 85 percent of these should be from primary sources. If you aren't seeing this volume of guns coming down the pipeline, you aren't working your sources hard enough. If you are seeing this kind of volume, week in and week out, and you can't make the deals at the TEK-I level, you need to look at the reasons. Is it strictly price? Is it your approach, your hours, your insistence on paying by check? In other words, is it something besides the offer price that you can correct without cutting your margins? Because if it is something else, moving to TEK-II won't help.

Now, after all is said and done, if you do move up to the TEK-II level, all of the elements of good gun trading become even more important. Selling at a price that gives the proper return is fairly straightforward, but it is really very easy to hold the inventory too long . . . not because it won't sell, but because you didn't get around to selling it. You didn't get the ad into the paper this week, or you didn't get the photos taken for the online auction, or you didn't get the gun shipped out to the repair shop. Days can quickly add up, and this is where you miss the turns target.

To counter this, I've found it very helpful to actually track the number of days a particular piece of inventory is on hand. This is actually no extra work, because in order to calculate my annualized return, I have to figure this anyway.

"Average inventory days" is calculated by counting the number of days each gun was in stock, and adding these totals for all of the guns sold. Divide this total by the number of guns sold and you have the average number of days your inventory was in stock. The easiest way to compute the days between date of purchase and date of sale is to record each date in the YYDDD format, where YY is the last two digits of the year, and DDD is the day of the year, from 001 to 366. Using this format, you can simply subtract the buy date from the sell date and get the number of days the stock was held.

For example, "days held" for a gun bought on January 2, 2005 (05002) and sold on August 31, 2005 (05243) would be 05243-05002=241 days. If the buy and sell dates are in different years, subtract another 634 days for each year between buy and sell dates. If the buy date is December 30, 2005 (05364) and the sell date is January 10, 2006 (06010), "days held" would be 06010-05364-634=12. If you are still reading this at the end of 2099, the technique works at century end by using all four digits of the year. And if you still have guns on hand that were purchased during the 20th century, just sell them right now . . . the number of days they've been held doesn't matter any more!

36. THE WANT LIST

I've mentioned your "want list" a couple of times, but just what is it? A good want list can make a major contribution to your success as a gun trader if it has the right information in it. Of course, you need current contract information, including at least the potential buyer's name and phone number. In addition, you'll want specific information related to what the customer wants. "A 30/06 bolt rifle" doesn't limit the field very much, and it suggests that this will be a one-shot deal . . . provided he hasn't already gotten the gun elsewhere. If you spoke to him yesterday, this "want" is probably still valid. So you'll want to identify the date of the information, or the date you last verified it. Entries such as "engraved American small-gauge doubles" is more interesting, but not necessarily more helpful. The more detail you have on make and model, the better. If you're trying to help him fill a collection, keep a list of what he has and doesn't have.

There are two ways to use your list. The first approach is to find something on the list, decide on a selling price, and then contact the potential buyer for confirmation before you make the purchase. This protects you from winding up holding a gun you wouldn't otherwise have bought. On the other hand, if you really know your customer's wants, and really trust him, you can use the list to purchase on the presumption that he will go along with your selection and pricing. Tread very carefully here until you build a real rapport with your customer, especially if he is looking for material not generally in demand.

It is extremely important to keep your list current. Many gun traders touch base with their best customers several times a month. Mind you, in return, a customer has a right to expect you to find goodies for him. He doesn't expect them for free, but he or she does expect to see potential purchases fairly frequently. At a minimum, refresh your list monthly, particularly if you will be buying without a specific commitment from a customer. Keep a detailed list, and keep it up to date. ∎

FINAL THOUGHTS

Well, there you have it . . . the what, why and how of gun trading. Now it's up to you. How well you do depends on how faithfully you follow the TEK system and how successfully you discipline yourself to stay cool, calm and collected while passing judgment on all the guns that will come your way.

I hope you will learn to enjoy this game as much as I do. Remember, there are other things in life besides gun trading, but most of them aren't nearly as much fun.

To all of you, good luck, good health, and good gun trading.

APPENDIX

A. LENGTHENING SHOTGUN CHAMBERS

Reprinted with permission from *Brownells Measuring*
& Rechambering Shotgun Chambers
by Ralph Walker
Photos and drawings by Ralph Walker

WARNING: Never attempt to disassemble or reassemble a firearm unless you are absolutely certain that it is empty and unloaded. Visually inspect the chamber, the magazine and the firing mechanism to be completely sure that no ammunition remains in the firearm.

Disassembly and reassembly should follow manufacturers' instructions. If such instructions are not immediately on hand, contact the manufacturer to see if they are available. If they are not available, consult other reference sources, such as books or persons with sufficient knowledge. If alternative sources are not available and you have a need to disassemble or reassemble the firearm, base your procedures on common sense and experience with similarly constructed firearms.

With regard to the use of these tools, the advice of Brownells, Inc. is more or less generic. For instructions about a specific application, it is best to seek out other sources and not rely solely on the general information and warnings the company provides.

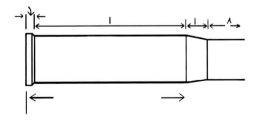

Standard shotgun chamber with short forcing cone.

SHOTGUN CHAMBER LENGTHS

The shotgun chamber consists of three sections. Starting at the rear is the recess cut for the rim of the shell. Next is the chamber body cut with a slight taper to assist inserting the shotgun shell and to provide for easy extraction after firing. Third is the forcing cone, beginning where the chamber body ends and tapering down to the bore section of the barrel.

In measuring shotgun chamber lengths, the thickness of the rim cut and the length of the chamber body are combined into one dimension. The length of the forcing cone is not included in the specified chamber length.

Prior to around 1900, shotgun chamber lengths varied considerably from manufacturer to manufacturer, often resulting in odd fractions. After 1900, shotguns have been produced in the following common chamber lengths:

GAUGE	CHAMBER LENGTH	GAUGE	CHAMBER LENGTH
10	2 7/8", 3 1/2"	20	2 1/2", 2 3/4", 3"
12	2", 2 1/2", 2 5/8", 2 3/4", 3"	28	2 3/4", 2 7/8"
16	2 9/16", 2 3/4"	.410	2", 2 1/2", 3"

NOTE: Other gauges produced or imported, but not in any great quantity, included the 8 Gauge (3", 3 1/8", 3 1/4"), 14 Gauge (2 9/16"), 24 Gauge (2 1/2"), 32 Gauge (2 1/2"), and 9mm (1 1/8", 1 9/16").

From 1920 to the mid-1930s the gauges were somewhat standardized to the following current chamber lengths:

GAUGE	CHAMBER LENGTH	GAUGE	CHAMBER LENGTH
10	3 1/2"	20	2 3/4", 3"
12	2 3/4", 3", 3 3/4"	28	2 3/4"
16	2 3/4"	.410	3"

NOTE: Ammunition is still produced in the 10 Gauge, 2 7/8" length. The .410 Gauge, 2 1/2" shell is also still produced, and a few special skeet guns are chambered in this length.

Metric chamber lengths and chamber diameter specifications are not exact duplicates of the current American specifications, since the accepted procedure is to carry the dimension to the nearest millimeter. The dimensions are usually stamped on the bottom of the barrel under the chamber. For example, 12-70. The 12 designates the gauge and the 70 designates the length of the chamber in millimeters. In this case, the 70mm is the equivalent of the American 2 3/4" chamber. Actually, 2 3/4" is exactly 69.85mm, but this small difference can be ignored for all practical purposes. The accepted conversion of metric chamber lengths to American standard chamber lengths is:

METRIC	INCHES	METRIC	INCHES
50	2″	73	2 7/8″
63-64	2 1/2″	76	3″
65	2 9/16″, 2 3/4″	89	3 1/2″
70	2 3/4″		

THE SHOTGUN SHELL
IN RELATION TO CHAMBER LENGTH

The unfired shotgun shell is considerably shorter than the chamber length. For example, the modern star crimped 20-gauge, 2 1/2″ shell is 2.44″ in length when loaded. When fired, the crimped end unfolds and the shell is then 2.75″ in length. This usually matches the chamber length of 2.75″. Therefore, the end of the fired shell case stops where the forcing cone begins tapering the chamber diameter down to the smaller bore diameter.

An unfired 20-gauge, 3″ shell measures 2.68″ in length, which allows it to easily enter the 20-gauge 2 3/4″ chamber (2.75″). However, when the 3″ shell is fired, the case unfolds to its full 3″ length. The extra .25″ of case body enters the forcing cone, creating a "bottleneck" effect which the shot and wads must pass.

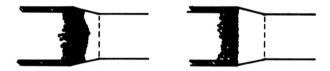

The "bottleneck" effect when the end of the fired shell case enters the forcing cone, thus squeezing and deforming the shot (left), as opposed to a correct length chamber (right) in which the fired case does not enter the forcing cone. Dotted line is the beginning of the bore and the end of the forcing cone.

The amount and type of powder loaded in a shell is carefully selected to provide the correct burning rate, which provides the pressure necessary to overcome the inertia of the shot, push it and the wads through the forcing cone, up the bore and through the choke. This balance is absolutely essential for good patterns and the overall correct function of the shotgun. Any time part of the fired shotgun case enters the forcing cone and creates the "bottleneck" effect, the balance is changed and several detrimental effects occur.

First, the momentary slowing of the shot charge by the "bottleneck" increases the rate of burning of the powder, which results in increased chamber pressure. In some cases, it is about the same as firing a proof-load shell. This excess pressure not only puts a strain on the gun's mechanism and barrel, but also increases the amount of recoil. Provided the mechanism is capable of safely withstanding the 10 percent to 25 percent increase in chamber pressure, the gun will slowly, but surely, be battered to pieces.

The second effect is that as the shot is forced through the "bottleneck," individual pellets become deformed and out of round. When the deformed pellets leave the barrel, they will not stay with the main charge as air pressure against them causes the deformed pellets to veer away from the mass of shot. The end result is a poorer pattern, both in percent and distribution of the pellets in the pattern circle.

While this may be an extreme example, it illustrates the necessity of having the chamber length correctly match the length of the fired shotgun shell. Any time a portion of the fired shell case enters the forcing cone, it decreases the efficiency of the barrel and consequently, the efficiency of the shotgun's performance.

USING YOUR CHAMBER DEPTH GAUGES

The chamber must be clean for accurate gauging. If normal cleaning procedures fail, make a special tool by using a brass bore brush and the forward section of a shotgun cleaning rod inserted in a 1/4″ electric hand drill. The rapid rotation of the bore brush will usually get the job done. If this fails, wrap a small amount of four ought (0000) steel wool around the bore brush and allow the drill to run for about a minute. Use both of these systems dry. They will remove the caked rust, powder residue, etc., and not damage the chamber. Wipe the chamber with a clean patch and use a strong light directed into the chamber to assure cleanliness before gauging.

Your gauges are machined to the specifications of each shotgun-gauge chamber dimension, as established by the Sporting Arms and Ammunition Manufacturers' Institute (SAAMI). The diameter of the front end is that of the chamber body where it meets the forcing cone; while a small bevel is cut on the front end to protect it, care should be exercised to prevent the edge from becoming nicked to avoid false gauging.

The forward edge of the circular cut around the gauge body is the point of the chamber length. This index edge should align with the rear of the chamber rim recess cut in the barrel if the chamber length is correct. Visual observation is easy but can be made more pronounced by filling the groove with a contrasting color. A simple method is to wipe the cut clean, then fill the groove with a white Lacquer-Stik. Another method is to use ordinary fingernail polish.

Lathe-cut grooves accurately indicate chamber length when placed in a clean chamber. The forward groove measures 2 3/4″ chambers, the rearward groove measures 3″ chambers.

The gauge body is not tapered as is the shotgun chamber to avoid false gauging on the side of the chamber. The rear end of the gauge is threaded 1/2"-20 tpi to accept the #080-546-501 Chamber Gauge Handle. A common 1/2"-20 bolt or threaded rod extension can also be used to allow easy insertion and extraction of the gauge in a chamber.

The handle is almost a necessity on pump or autoloader barrels with long barrel extensions. After use, wipe the gauge clean and lightly oil. Store the gauges separately.

Chamber depth gauge inserted in 12-gauge, 3" chamber, with pointer indicating that the gauge shows proper chamber depth, or length, for 3" chamber.

SHORT CHAMBERS

Starting around 1930, it became standard practice to stamp both the gauge and the chamber length on the barrel, such as "12-Gauge, 2 3/4"" or an abbreviation. While there are exceptions to the rule, a barrel stamped with only the gauge specifications should be checked with the chamber-length gauge. Chances are that the chamber length is shorter than the current standard. It is good practice to also check metric marked chambers to assure correct dimensions for American shells.

.410 Gauge: The majority of pumps and semi-automatics will be chambered for the 3" shell, as Winchester pioneered this field in the 1930s with their Model 42 pump. Prior to that time the .410 was chambered in the 2 1/2" length or the earlier 2" length. The designation .410 is somewhat misleading; it is the bore diameter expressed in hundredths of an inch and not the gauge as measured for other shotguns. Some early single and double barrels were marked either 12mm or 67 gauge.

28 Gauge: The original 1903 version of this shell was in 2 7/8" chamber length but was standardized in the 1920s to the current 2 3/4" chamber length. The longer 2 7/8" chamber will present no problems with the current 2 3/4" shell, but the condition of the gun should be carefully considered in shooting the 2 3/4" magnum shell with one ounce of shot, since the earlier guns were designed for a light load and three-quarters of an ounce of shot. A few European doubles, although stamped for the 2 3/4" shell, will give extraction problems with American shells, as the chambers are extremely tight, especially in the ultra-light version guns. Any that do not accept the 2 3/4″ gauge can be re-chambered to eliminate the problem. NOTE: There were a few guns chambered for a special 2 3/4″, 28-gauge shell, but these are extremely rare.

20 Gauge: Up until 1926, the standard chamber length was 2 1/2″, and a considerable number of guns will be found with this chamber length. Provided the barrel and the gun mechanism are in good condition, these guns can often be re-chambered to current 2 3/4″ length. Single and double barrels require only re-chambering, but the pumps and semi-automatics will usually require alterations of the feed mechanism and ejection ports in the receiver. Prior to World War I, a few double barrels and one pump were chambered for the 3″ shell loaded with 1 1/8 oz. of shot. It was not popular. But after World War II, the 3″ shell was increased to 1 1/8 oz. of shot, and it has rapidly gained in popularity. Conversion from the 2 3/4″ chamber to the 3″ chamber is usually safe in well-built guns, but under no circumstance should a 2 1/2″ chamber be converted to the 3″ chamber.

16 Gauge: The 2 9/16″ chamber length was both the American and the European standard until 1929, when the American standard was changed to the current 2 3/4″ length. The European standard did not change until after World War II, and even today, the 2 9/16″ (65mm) is still popular in some sections of Europe. The popularity of the gauge, the large number of guns manufactured in the U.S. prior to 1929, and the vast array of imports both before and after World War II, have resulted in literally thousands of 16-gauge, 2 9/16″ guns still in use. In fact, only in recent years have the ammunition manufacturers discontinued production of 2 9/16″ shells. Conversion of single and double barrels to the 2 3/4″ chamber seldom requires more than re-chambering. Pumps and semi-automatics will require alterations of the mechanism. While any sound gun will accept the conversion, the use of short magnum shells should be avoided.

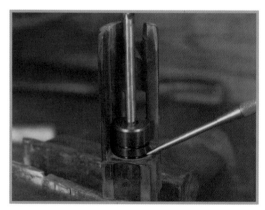

A chamber gauge verifies that the chamber in this 12-gauge auto barrel is 2 3/4", measuring to the forward (or 2 3/4") ring in the gauge. Note the chamber gauge handle on the gauge.

12 Gauge: This is, without a doubt, the most popular gauge in shotguns, and it has been produced in the widest variety of chamber lengths. The British still make an ultra-light upland game gun in the 2″ chamber length and prefer the 2 1/2″ shell and chamber length for general use. The 2 3/4″ chamber and shell are considered appropriate for heavy use. A considerable number of the 2 1/2″ chambered guns have been imported, and the length was popular in the early 1930s, with some American doubles being produced in this length.

Classic example of a short chamber. After thorough cleaning, it will not accept the gauge to a full 2 3/4" depth. This particular chamber measured 2 5/8" prior to re-chambering.

The 2 5/8″ chamber length was standard in the U.S. until the mid-1920s, when the 2 3/4″ chamber was adopted. The 3″ chamber length and shell began in the 1930s and have steadily gained popularity due to the availability of heavy 1 7/8 oz. loading, which almost matches the 10-gauge, 3 1/2″, 2-oz. load.

Rechambering of the 2″ and 2 1/2″ chambers to the current 2 3/4″ chamber length should be approached with caution due to the light weight of the guns.

The 2 5/8″ chamber length is more commonly encountered than realized as many manufacturers obviously did not make the change when the 2 3/4″ chamber was adopted. Any barrel that is not stamped 2 3/4″ should be gauged. The conversion to 2 3/4″ length should present no problems if the gun is in good condition, and it will increase the performance of the gun.

The rechambering of a current 2 3/4″ chamber or the older 2 5/8″ chamber length to the 3″ chamber length is of questionable safety, regardless of the condition of the barrel or gun mechanism. Even if successful, the heavy-loaded 3″ shell with 1 7/8 oz. of shot will generally batter a gun mechanism to uselessness. Older guns should definitely not be rechambered to the new 3 1/2″ magnum.

10 Gauge: This has been made in two chamber lengths, 2 7/8″ and the current 3 1/2″. Under no circumstances should a 2 7/8″ chamber be converted to the 3 1/2″ chamber length.

NOTES ON CONVERSION

As stated, single- and double-barrel guns can normally be converted to the longer chambers with little effort other than rechambering. Some of the doubles with automatic ejectors may require retiming of the ejectors, but generally no special technique is required. The Browning Five Shot Semi-automatic in 16-gauge, 2 9/16″ chamber length is quite common, but requires the alteration of parts internally for proper operation with the 2 3/4″ length shell.

Malfunctions are usually the result of not making the full conversion as recommended by Browning. The step-by-step conversion in full detail can be found on pages 240-242 of *Brownells Encyclopedia of Modern Firearms.* Follow the directions carefully and the gun should function perfectly. It is recommended that the short magnum 16-gauge shells not be used in a converted Browning as the gun was not designed for this heavy load. The conversion of pumps such as the Winchester Model 1912 in short chambers follows the same basic procedure.

The same chamber as shown in the last photo, still prior to rechambering, easily accepts an unfired 2 3/4″ shell. However, when fired, this shell will protrude into the forcing cone area, causing excessive pressures, recoil, and damage to the gun. Following these photos, this gun was rechambered to 2 3/4″.

THE LONG FORCING CONE

The example of firing a 3″ shell in a 2 3/4″ length chamber and the resulting effects are, in varying degrees, true with all short chambers. It is also true to a lesser degree with chambers of the correct length, but with the forcing cone of the chamber cut to accommodate the old roll-type crimped shells. These forcing cones are short and abrupt, with a length of one-half-inch about average.

The old roll-type crimped paper shotgun shells had a heavy piece of cardboard, commonly termed the nitro wad, directly over the powder charge in the shell. Next came the felt filler wads, then the shot charge, and finally the over shot wad with the shotgun case end rolled over to hold the wad in place.

When fired, the pressure from the powder pushed the roll crimp straight as the wad and shot column moved out of the shell. It was important that the powder gas not be allowed to pass around the wads and disrupt the shot. For this reason, the forcing cone was short and abrupt to engage the over powder nitro immediately as it left the shell. It was compressed by the forcing cone and held the gas pressure behind the wad.

The invention of plastic, cup-shaped, over powder wads was a giant step forward. As gas pressure increased, it automatically pressed the cup edge firmly outward for a perfect gas seal. Its superiority over the paper nitro wad can best be judged by the fact that reloading manuals recommended decreasing the powder charge 10 percent when the plastic-cup wad was used instead of the nitro paper wad.

The plastic-cup powder wad completely replaced the nitro wad. Next came the plastic shot protector and then the plastic filler wads. The final step was the joining of all three components into one unit. This unit perfectly seals the gas pressure, cushions the impact of getting the shot moving, and protects the shot from being rubbed against the sides of the bore and deformed. Replacement of the old waxed-paper shell and one-piece wad has resulted in a shotgun shell far superior in every way to the old shell.

CONVERTING OLD FORCING CONES TO THE LONG FORCING CONE

Fired in a barrel from which all choke has been removed, the modern plastic shell will generally produce a five percent to 10 percent better pattern at a given distance than a similarly loaded shell using the old wads, no shot protector, over shot wad, etc. In a choked barrel, the new shell has the effect of increasing pattern performance approximately a half to a full degree of choke. In other words, a barrel choked modified and intended for the old type shells will produce either an improved modified or a full-choke pattern with the new shell.

The 30″ circle at 40 yards has always been the method of determining the efficiency of a full-choked barrel. With a barrel chambered and choked for the old type shell, 70 percent is considered a good pattern. Yet 30 percent of the shot is not in the circle and, consequently, has been lost for practical purposes. The new type shell will increase the percent to 75 or 80, thus utilizing more of the shot that was in the shell before it was fired. This is accomplished primarily by reducing pellet deformation as the pellets travel through the forcing cone and barrel.

Patterning a shotgun at the range where it will be used will tell you much more about the performance your customer wants than sticking to the old, standard 40-yard system. The performance of an improved cylinder barrel at 40 yards is not a guarantee of performance at the shorter ranges for which the improved cylinder is intended. The ultimate barrel will produce the desired pattern, completely without open spaces or "free holes," at the distance for which the degree of choke was intended.

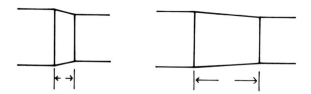

This illustrates, in proportion, the difference between the two types of forcing cones. While there are variations, of course, the dimensions shown are average.

The short and abrupt forcing cone always deformed some of the shot as it was pushed through the short cone, but this was a necessity with the old-type shell. It is not a necessity with the modern unit and folded-crimp plastic shell. In fact, it actually decreases the efficiency of the new shell! With modern shells, a longer forcing cone allows the shot to pass from the chamber to the smaller bore diameter with less shot being deformed, and without the gas-leak problem.

Forcing cones from 1" to 3" in length have been tested and the results indicate that generally a forcing cone of approximately 1 1/2" in length will provide the best results with the widest variety of loads. A short forcing cone barrel recut to the long forcing cone may give a five percent to 10 percent pattern increase both in density and pellet distribution. The actual pattern percent gain will vary with individual barrels, gauges, pellet sizes and shell loads used. However, the combination of the long forcing cone and the modern shell will invariably produce a more efficient pattern.

An additional advantage of the long forcing cone is that the plastic shell body sometimes unfolds and stretches to a length longer than specified. In a 2 3/4" chamber, the length can be as much as 2.9" instead of the correct 2 3/4". The stretching varies with the quality of the shell and the load. Cheap short magnum shells will stretch more than a quality skeet- or trap-load shell. In the short and abrupt forcing cone, this stretching allows the end of the shell to enter the forcing cone and create the "bottleneck" effect similar to a short chamber, and with similar results.

RECUTTING FORCING CONES AND CHAMBERS

Brownells Long Forcing Cone Reamers can be used to extend the forcing cone from the original short configuration, and under some conditions, may also be used to lengthen early short chambers to accept modern standard and low-velocity loaded shells.

As a general rule we encourage the use of a good quality chamber reamer for the actual cutting of the chamber. Safety should always be given first priority when rechambering any firearm. The acceptable conversion should never be attempted without a thorough examination of the condition of the gun and its components. A gun in good condition, with all components locking and functioning correctly can normally be safely converted.

Yet similar models in poor condition, with parts and components worn and loose, should not be converted. Always remember that with older model guns the magnum load of its day is probably the accepted field load of today. For this reason, caution should be exercised to select only field or target loads and avoid the current heavy short magnum shell loads. If in doubt about the safety of rechambering a particular gun . . . DON'T!

The Brownells Long Forcing Cone Reamers are available in two different forms: the traditional straight flute and the more modern helical or spiral flute. Spiral flute reamers function with a shearing cut, which under some conditions can be more efficient than the cutting action of a straight-fluted reamer. Both can be used in the same manner and both, when used properly, will normally leave a very smooth surface. They are exclusively manufactured for us by one of the country's oldest reamer suppliers.

Be sure the reamer cutting edges are kept sharp by careful stoning with a hard Arkansas stone. When in use, the metal chips from the removed metal should be equal in front of every cutting edge to assure that the reamer is cutting evenly on all sides. If the chip build-up is in front of only one or two flutes, the other flutes are not cutting. Stone the face of these flutes lightly until the metal removal equalizes. DO NOT stone the tops of the flutes.

Barrel in vise, chamber end up, with reamer in position to begin cutting new chamber.

T-handle wrench gives control for accurate reaming.

NOTE: On some guns, the original chamber diameter will not match the modern SAAMI specifications of the reamer. If it is smaller than the reamer, the reamer will open up the forward end of the chamber to the nominal chamber-mouth dimension used in a modern chamber. If the original chamber is larger in diameter than today's specifications show, the reamer will leave a slight step. This step normally will not cause function problems. A little extra time spent honing the chamber and forcing cone will "blend" the step into the chamber, but that is only needed for cosmetic reasons.

We have observed that barrel steels used on shotguns vary greatly in hardness. Some steels will cut easily with little effort, while others require much greater force and will try to start "chattering" with any cutter used. Even, downward pressure on the reamer and plenty of cutting oil, will usually minimize or eliminate this chatter. If it persists into the finished forcing cone length, you have no choice but to spend extra time with the barrel hone to clean up the chatter marks.

The actual length of the finished long forcing cone will vary due to the actual bore diameter of the barrel. The same reamer used in a barrel with a .725″ diameter bore will give a longer forcing cone than if it is used in a barrel with a .740″ bore. This is important to remember:

The angle of the forcing cone is the same in both barrels, and it is the longer, gentler angle that reduces shot deformation in the forcing cone!

Place the barrel in a padded vise, with the chamber toward the ceiling and the breech end as low as possible for observation and ease of cutting. Squirt cutting oil into the chamber and onto the flutes of the reamer, as the oil will help achieve a smooth cut. While the wrench used to turn the reamer should be secure to the reamer, it is necessary to exert pressure equally, allowing the tapered reamer to "feel" its own way and keep centered. Side pressure on the handle can result in an oval chamber.

After about two or three complete revolutions of the reamer, remove it straight up and out of the chamber. Wipe away all metal chips and cutting oil from the reamer (an old toothbrush and mineral spirits work fine for this job). Next, run a dry patch through the bore to remove any lingering chips and cutting oil. Check with your chamber depth gauge.

Regardless of the number of times, it is important that the rechambering be done slowly, the reamer and barrel cleaned each time, and the depth constantly checked with the gauge. A strong light directed into the chamber will help you see the progress of the rechambering, and you can quickly note if you are not turning the reamer with even strokes.

If initial gauging has indicated correct chamber length but the chamber has the short, abrupt forcing cone and you want to rechamber for the long forcing cone, the procedure is identical, with two variations.

First, all traces of the old forcing cone must be removed. Second, to achieve this, the chamber must be cut slightly longer than standard, as many of the old forcing cones are pitted. The front edge of the circular cut grooves around the gauge body is the index point for correct chamber length. However, it will generally be necessary to use the REAR edge of the circular cut on the gauge as the index point for chamber depth, in order to remove all of the old forcing cone. This extra length will not affect the barrel performance, as 2 3/4″ shells are commonly fired in 3″ chamber length 20- and 12-gauge shotguns.

Finish the rechambering job by polishing the chamber and new forcing cone with a 500-grit aluminum oxide cloth. The Brownell "Choke Hone" tool will do the job faster and with more even results. You use this rotating tool, dry, for about one minute of revolution in an electric hand drill to remove any roughness, then squirt cutting oil up into the chamber and use the tool for about two minutes more. The result will be a highly polished forcing cone.

CONCLUSION

The ultimate goal is to achieve as close to 100 percent of the pellets as possible striking within the 30″ pattern circle, with the pellets evenly distributed. The ammunition manufacturers have provided one giant step forward toward this goal with modern shotgun shells. Using these shells in chambers of correct depth is another step forward. The long forcing cone is still another step toward that goal.

There is a fourth step available: reworking the choke to achieve the maximum percent of pellets evenly distributed in the 30″ circle at the desired range.

Brownells "Choke Set" was introduced many years ago, and thousands of gun shops across the country will testify to its effectiveness in improving shotgun patterns. By combining the modern shotgun, correct chamber length, long forcing cone and correct choke dimensions, you can achieve the maximum efficiency of any barrel, regardless of age or model of gun.

These directions reproduced courtesy of Brownells, Incorporated, Montezuma, Iowa. © 2003 Brownells, Inc.

B. MAKING CHAMBER CASTS WITH CERROSAFE™

WARNING: To help avoid injury, be sure to wear proper clothing when working with any high-temperature heat source, such as an oxyacetylene torch or gas burner. Always wear protective gloves, a long-sleeve cotton or wool shirt, pull-on high-top leather boots, and a full face shield along with appropriate safety glasses or goggles. Remove all flammable material from your work area and keep a fully charged fire extinguisher within reach.

With regard to the use of these tools, the advice of Brownells, Inc. is generic. For instructions about a specific application, it is best to seek out other sources and not rely solely on the general information and warnings the company provides.

Cerrosafe casting is used any time a "positive" copy must be made of a rifle, shotgun or handgun chamber, neck, throat or bore. Chamber casts are used to determine the caliber of an unknown or unmarked firearm, and to verify the marked caliber if it is suspected that the original chamber has been altered. It is also used to check dimensions and condition of the neck, throat and bore to help determine bullet fit and cans neck turning requirements.

Cerrosafe shrinks slightly during initial cooling. It then expands to the chamber's original size about one hour after cooling to room temperature. After cooling for about 200 hours, the chamber cast will expand about .0025″ over the actual chamber size. Cerrosafe is completely reusable; the chamber cast can be re-melted and reused after all necessary measurements have been taken.

Cerrosafe can also be used to help remove stuck cartridge cases were the extractor has pulled the head from the case bode, leaving the front of the case lodged in the chamber.

WARNING: The state of California has acknowledged that Cerrosafe contains a chemical that may cause cancer, birth defects, and other reproductive harm.

HOW TO USE CERROSAFE

Cerrosafe has a melting range from 158 degrees to 190 degrees Fahrenheit. (Note: Overheating may cause separation of the components of Cerrosafe alloy.) Melt Cerrosafe in a double boiler or other means of clean, indirect heat. It should be poured from a clean ladle. If using a heavy iron bullet-caster's or plumber's ladle, a propane torch with a low flame can be used to heat the ladle from the bottom until the Cerrosafe is completely molten. A tin can may also be used as a ladle, with the lip bent to form a pouring spout, and locking pliers (such as Visegrip brand) used as a handle. If a small can is used, it should be set on a piece of heavy sheet steel and the heat applied to the steel from underneath with a propane torch. An industrial hot-air gun can also be used to heat the Cerrosafe in a pouring ladle.

Disassemble the firearm as needed to gain access to the chamber. To cast a chamber on a gun that does not allow ready access to the chamber (a bolt or lever action rifle for example), you must make a pouring tube and pour the molten Cerrosafe through the tube to reach the chamber. Tubes can be made of steel, brass or aluminum tubing and should have a piece of material flared into a funnel at the upper end. Keep the tube as short as possible so the molten Cerrosafe will not solidify inside it. You many need an assistant to hold the tube with a pair of pliers and direct the flame of a propane torch over the tube to keep the Cerrosafe from solidifying inside during the pour.

The barrel and chamber must be clean and dry before you pour. Insert a tight-fitting cotton cleaning patch on a jag into the bore from the muzzle to serve as a "dam" ahead of the throat of the chamber. Heat the barrel at the chamber just to the point where it is uncomfortable to hold with your bare hand.

Heat the Cerrosafe as directed above and carefully pour it into the chamber until it shows a slight mound at the rear of the chamber. Excess Cerrosafe at the rear of the chamber can sometimes prevent removal of the chamber cast. If this happens, melt the Cerrosafe in the chamber with a propane torch on the barrel and pour it back into the ladle.

After the Cerrosafe has solidified, the cast can be pushed out of the chamber. We recommend using a nylon-covered steel cleaning rod with a brass jag tip. Push out the Cerrosafe chamber cast within one-half hour after casting. If more than one hour elapses before you attempt to remove the chamber cast, the Cerrosafe will start to expand and will have to be re-melted and allowed to cool in the chamber to remove it.

To remove the chamber cast from the chamber, clamp the barreled action horizontally in a padded bench vise and tap the handle of the cleaning rod with the palm of your hand to start the cast free from the chamber. Remove the barreled action from the vise and hold the breech end over a folded towel or shop rag on your bench top. Finish pushing out the chamber cast carefully so that it emerges from the action onto the folded cloth. Although the chamber cast will be relatively hard, it can be damaged if dropped onto a hard surface, such as an unpadded bench top or the floor.

Revolver chambers can be successfully cast with Cerrosafe if a plate of smooth, hard material, such as aluminum or Masonite, is clamped over the front of the chamber mouth. Be sure to cut a clearance hole for any gas ring or bearing surface at the crane or center pin location on the cylinder. Disassemble the cylinder as completely as possible. Remove the extractor star from double-action revolver cylinders.

REMOVING BROKEN CARTRIDGE CASES FROM CHAMBERS

Occasionally, a combination of factors will cause the head of a cartridge case to separate from the body of the case during firing. If the chamber or the exterior of the cartridge is dirty or corroded, it can be extremely difficult to remove the broken cartridge without damaging the chamber. Cerrosafe can usually help you extract the front of the case without causing further damage to the chamber.

Clean the inside of the case with the correctly sized, dry, bronze chamber brush. Insert a tight-fitting cotton cleaning patch (on the jag) into the bore from the muzzle, to serve as a "dam" for the Cerrosafe. Push the cleaning patch into the bore to within 1/2″ of the mouth of the broken cartridge case.

Melt and pour Cerrosafe into the chamber as described above. It is not necessary to make a mound of Cerrosafe at the chamber mouth as you would to measure an unknown chamber. When the Cerrosafe has cooled to room temperature (or one-half hour, maximum), use your cleaning rod to push out the broken cartridge case.

In extreme situations, you may have to use a bore-fitting brass rod in place of the cleaning, and use a brass or plastic-faced hammer to start the broken cartridge case from the chamber. After the case has been removed, the Cerrosafe can be re-melted and reused.

Once the broken cartridge case has been removed, be sure to inspect both the rifle and the ammunition to determine the probable cause of the broken cartridge case. In some instances, the case separation may have been caused by excessive headspace. Some case head separations result from either incorrect ammunition or improperly loaded ammunition being used.

CAUTION: Cerrosafe should not be used to make a chamber cast if you suspect the chamber is bulged, badly pitted, or scored, or if the throat diameter is eroded larger than the chamber mouth. In these instances, the chamber cast will become "mechanically locked" into the chamber because of over-aging. If this happens, secure the barrel in a padded bench vise with the breech end pointing up. Plug the bore as above and use a propane torch or heat gun to heat the barrel's breech and re-melt the Cerrosafe. Allow the chamber cast to cool to room temperature (no more than one-half hour) before attempting to remove as described above.

A FEW FINAL WORDS ON MEASURING CHAMBER CASTS

When Cerrosafe is used to determine chamber dimensions for identification of unknown chambers, remember you must allow for the expansion of the cast. Published dimensions for cartridges are usually based on measured examples of the cartridges, and a sample of several "identical" cartridges from different lots or from different manufacturers may vary significantly.

Also, don't forget that a chamber will almost always be several thousandths of an inch larger in all dimensions than the cartridge to allow for proper feeding and functioning. Manufacturing tolerances of chamber reamers must be taken into account. With many bolt-action rifles and some pumps and auto-loaders, you will not be able to make a cast of the complete chamber, including the rim section, since the bolt face is set back from the breech of the barrel.

These directions reproduced courtesy of Brownells, Incorporated, Montezuma Iowa. © 2004 Brownells, Inc. ∎

NOTES

NOTES

NOTES

NOTES